Khrennikov

**L. Grigoryev
and Y. Platek**

Translated by Yuri Sviridov

PAGANINIANA PUBLICATIONS, INC.
211 West Sylvania Avenue, Neptune City, New Jersey 07753

CONTENTS

Foreword

... A hot June afternoon in 1982. A group of conductors, actors, stage managers and directors, a few dozen of them all told, gathered in a small rehearsal hall. The brilliant sunshine flooded the room making it look bright and gay. Now and then the boom of the traffic outside intruded itself upon the quiet conversation in the room. Suddenly the babble of voices died down as a composer whose face was well familiar to everyone present briskly came into the room. He shook hands with everyone flashing a friendly smile and joking about the sweltering weather. Then he took off his jacket, sat down at the piano, loosened the collar of his shirt and with a shy, soft smile began to play, singing as he went along. Little by little as he identified himself more and more with his characters, at times seeking to represent a whole orchestra, the composer got carried away, infecting his audience with his enthusiasm. Enchanted by the music, everybody was now quite oblivious of the traffic noise.

... On that occasion Tikhon Khrennikov was presenting his latest musical to members of the company and management of Moscow's Stanislavsky and Nemirovich-Danchenko Musical Theatre. His audience included both young actors and actresses and those of the older generation who had known the composer for years and even decades. And it could be that it was in the same room where back in the 1930s Tikhon Khrennikov had unveiled the first movement of his first opera *In Storm*. It was also here, within these walls, that Nemirovich-Danchenko, the famous man of the theatre, held his rehearsals with members of the cast of an opera that has since become a permanent item in the repertoire of opera houses all across the Soviet Union.

Khrennikov's career in music covers half a century. His was an eventful, action-packed life that saw notable musical events, heated arguments, ups and downs, joys and sorrows, and an impressive musical output. . . .

**Tikhon Khrennikov at the piano
in his study.**

And always, at all times, Tikhon Khrennikov was at the very center of the Soviet musical scene where passions often ran high. He was always in the thick of things keeping pace with the times.

By and large, he has lived a happy life in "big-time" music but by no means an unclouded one. It was never roses all the way, never a succession of triumphs and easy conquests of professional summits. Success, applause, recognition, fame . . . yes, all that was well earned. But did it all come without struggle, without setbacks and hurt pride, without losses? Of course not! This is how it might seem to an idle outside observer, perhaps. And yet, on balance, it was a happy life. It was also a rare kind of happiness, one that comes from the satisfaction of making the right choice, from a sense of loyalty to cherished ideals. A happiness that comes from the realization that you have stayed the course and served the cause you are totally committed to – a lifetime in the service of your country and its people.

Over the past fifty years we have heard so many conflicting opinions about him. So many heated arguments have flared up around his compositions in the past and some of his more recent works. Not a few lances have been broken over them by critics. Today, when Khrennikov is generally acknowledged as a leading light of Soviet music, his work is the subject of monographs and other musicological works and each bar of his scores has been carefully analyzed and evaluated for its true worth in numerous analytical studies. But objective descriptions tend to obscure the living image of Khrennikov, man and composer. They blur the true view of his role and place in the musical kaleidoscope of the 20th century.

Half a century . . . a long enough period by the standards of our fast-moving world. Are we always able to relate correctly and adequately the career of a major contemporary artist to the march of time with which he has always been careful to keep pace?

We thought it important to survey the life and times of this remarkable man. We also thought it interesting to look at Tikhon Khrennikov and his complex career through the eyes of the men and women who had lived and worked with him at different periods, who either shared his ideas or opposed them, to examine arguments for and against the man.

Hence the idea of writing this book.

Top: Khrennikov's career in music covers half a century. His has been an eventful, action-packed life . . .
Bottom: The street in the town of Yelets where Tikhon Khrennikov spent his childhood years. On the left, the small one-story house where the composer was born. "Not only Novgorod, Kiev, Vladimir but also the humble huts of Yelets . . . are curious relics of medieval Russian history."

Early Years

. . . Dear Mikhail Fabianovich,

I am sending you a few compositions by the boy I mentioned to you. . . . I am not sending everything he has written, the rest is still on the raw side and he does not want to show rough copies of anything (I refer to the shape they are in and not the content). He will show you the rest himself when he comes to Moscow. I am looking forward to your verdict. I want to help this boy so much. I may be mistaken but he does strike me as a very gifted lad. Once again I apologize for trespassing on your time. But if he is indeed talented I would like someone of your experience to give him guidance and set him on the right path.

From a letter to M.F. Gnesin from
S.G. Tseitlina.   Yelets, 23 December, 1927.

"My heart has forever retained the memory of those charming quiet streets and crooked lanes of Yelets, the old Russian town where I was born and grew up, of the placid river Sosna, of the town's orchards famous throughout Russia, and most important of all, of the stimulating musical atmosphere which reigned in our family. As far back as I can remember music was my dream. I did not immediately have the chance to take up serious musical studies but always knew that nothing else would ever attract me. Music was my first and only love, my only cherished dream and I never allowed myself even to think of betraying my dream . . ."

Yelets is one of the oldest towns in the central part of European Russia. The 800-year-old town stands on the Sosna River in a lovely scenic setting which has been celebrated by Turgenyev who was born and spent many years of his life in the neighboring Orel gubernia. This small ancient town has been through a lot. Karamzin, the great Russian historian, wrote in his *A History of the Russian State*, "not only Novgorod, Kiev, Vladimir but also the humble huts of Yelets, Kozelsk and Galich are curious relics of medieval Russian history."

The earliest mention of Yelets is contained in the Nikon chronicles of 1146. In those distant days Yelets was one of the fortress towns built to defend the southern borders of Old Rus from the frequent incursions of war-like nomadic tribes. As one of the frontier towns on the outer perimeter of Old Rus, Yelets, according to historian V.N. Tatishchev, "was an important strategic stronghold crucial to the defense of Russian lands." Early in the 19th century a chapel was put up in Yelets to commemorate those of its residents who fell in a 1395 battle with the hordes of Tamerlane. In many subsequent wars the sons of this fringe Russian land distinguished themselves by a display of remarkable valor and fortitude. Down the centuries Yelets was repeatedly razed to the ground and sacked but arose from the ashes like a phoenix each time. Bunin, the famous Russian writer who was a native of Yelets, wrote this in *The Lives of Arsenyev:* "The town was proud of its antiquity and with good reason: it was indeed one of the most Russian of ancient Russian towns. It stood amid the boundless black-earth fields of the sub-steppe zone, close to the fateful limit beyond which lay wild and unknown lands. Yelets was one of the vital fastnesses of Old Rus which, according to medieval chronicles, were the first to breathe in the smoke, the dust and the cold that swept in from beneath those ominous Asiatic storm clouds which gathered over them at frequent intervals; the first to see the sinister glow of those terrible fires which were started by the invaders by day and by night, the first to forewarn Moscow of an impending disaster and the first to fall in battle to save the capital city . . ."

By the start of the 20th century Yelets had grown into a fair-sized provincial town little different from many others in the middle of European Russia. It was a hard working town, too, at a time when the workers' movement in Russia was rapidly growing stronger. About a third of its population were factory workers. Yelets was also famous for its handicrafts. The exquisite products of its skillful lace-makers were popular throughout Russia. The people of Yelets were also fond of singing . . . Those folk singers who were immortalized by Turgenyev in his novels held their spontaneous contests in the villages of the neighboring gubernias. This blessed land has produced not a few talents who have made it famous. Among them are the pride of Russian letters: Turgenyev, Tyutchev, Fet, Leskov, Pisarev, Bunin, Prishvin . . . Some of them were born in these parts while others lived and worked here for long periods. All of them, each in his own way, celebrated the inimitable natural beauty of this part of Russia. Not only the scenic beauty of the place but the local way of life, folk arts and handicrafts also had a very special Russian quality about them, and had a poetry and music all their own.

Mitrofan Khrennikov, the composer's elder brother, recalls: "During the years of our childhood Yelets was a very musical town. A merry town. Its four public gardens and, more frequently, its parks were the focal points of spontaneous music-making provided by the combined efforts of the fire brigade's brass band and string orchestras. We boys were invariably drawn to these places. And of course we slipped in without any admission tickets or climbed over the fence. In the evening the sounds of music literally hovered over the town. People singing popular romances, folk and student songs could be heard all over the place."

This, coupled with the poetic beauty of the surrounding countryside,
the mellow melodies of folk songs and the sound atmosphere of a hard-
working town surrounded Tikhon Khrennikov from early childhood and
could not but leave a deep imprint on his impressionable soul. Those
were bright childhood impressions that remained with him throughout
his life. In a sense they helped shape his outlook and character. Another
major influence was the stimulating family atmosphere in which Tikhon
grew up.

Tikhon Khrennikov was born on 10 June 1913, the tenth child of a
close-knit family. His father Nikolai Ivanovich was a reserved and strict
head of the family whose saving grace was a gentle sense of humor. For
decades he had served as an agent for local merchants but his income was
barely enough to provide for the large family and give his children a decent education, something that had been denied him. His primary concern was to ensure that his children grew up to be honest, hard-working
people with a sense of dignity. His wife, Varvara Vasilyevna, looked after
the upbringing of the children.

15

The Khrennikovs were a gracious and hospitable lot who kept open house. Friends and relatives were welcome and frequent guests in the house and music was always played on such occasions. All sorts of instruments were played and folk songs and popular romances were staple items of the evening's entertainment. None of the performers were professionals but they more than made up for it by contributing to the proceedings with great enthusiasm, sincerity and skill. Several members of the family were expert hands at playing the mandolin and the guitar. Gleb, Tikhon's oldest brother, had a good tenor voice. As a boy he sang in the local church choir. Later he entered the Moscow Conservatory. Whenever he returned from Moscow, Gleb gave concerts in his home town. He would receive the warmest applause for his rendition of *Canio's Aria* from Leoncavallo's opera *Pagliacci* as well as for the romance *White and Pale* which was very popular in those days. Gleb certainly showed good promise as a singer. But the First World War interrupted his studies. Gleb was sent off to the front and was killed in action near Dvinsk early in 1918.

Tikhon, the youngest in the family, was not yet five at the time. But the anxieties of those years, the stormy events of the Revolution and the turmoil of the Civil War that followed left an indelible mark on his memory. He would recall later: "My childhood passed in the years of the Civil War. I remember the days when Denikin's army was approaching Yelets and the fierce fighting against Mamontov's cavalry, units of the so-called Caucasus Army and the roving bands of White Cossacks. I also remember vividly how we boys stood in the street and followed with admiring eyes a detachment of Red Cadets marching off to the front. My brother Nikolai was at the head of the column and I tried to keep pace mincing along beside him. I was so proud of my brother . . . The alarming tension of those days left a deep imprint on my heart as did also the quiet poetry of my peaceful home town and the sounds of music floating over the fragrant orchards in full bloom."

The world of music had an irresistible fascination for Tikhon. Tikhon was a curious, sensitive and very impressionable boy. He was an avid reader of books, and an enthusiastic participant in all the games. He was also an excellent swimmer and skier. Tikhon started school when he was only six. He was admitted as he could read and write quite well. He was also lucky to have Ivan Zyuzyukin for his first singing master. Zyuzyukin spotted and developed Tikhon's musical ability. He was, perhaps, the first in the long line of kind and responsive people whom, as Khrennikov would write later, he was fortunate to meet in the years that followed . . .

Tikhon had his first introduction to the mandolin and the guitar in early childhood. He was a fast learner and before long could play the guitar quite well. Later he joined his school's amateur orchestra which often played in the town's Luna Park. At one such concert Tikhon performed a solo on a strange contraption of his own invention: an "instrument" made of tumblers arranged in carefully selected series.

But Tikhon's great dream was always the piano. The Khrennikovs could not afford an expensive instrument like that and Tikhon had only touched the keyboard of the piano owned by friends of the family. After the war was over, life in the town was slowly getting back to normal. It was a new life, too. His father was getting on in years and so Tikhon's elder sister took over as the family's breadwinner. She taught in the local railway school, moonlighting as the school's librarian, initially without pay. But one day her pay was backdated and she received a lump sum. She decided to buy a secondhand piano to enable her younger sister and brother, Nina and Tikhon, to take piano lessons.

Tikhon Khrennikov and his little daughter Natalya.

Poster announcing a November 20, 1933 concert of works by "student composers of the Conservatory," including five piano pieces by Tikhon Khrennikov—performed by himself.

Konstantin Igumnov, pianist and pedagogue of unique talent, under whom Khrennikov's first tutor Vladimir Agarkov had studied piano.

Tikhon Khrennikov in his 'teens. "He was insatiably inquisitive about all things to do with music."

Around that time Tikhon was introduced to Kveton, a Czech musician who was living in Yelets. Kveton had lived in Russia long enough to regard himself as a Russian in everything but name. His father had been the Kapellmeister (resident conductor) of a military band and sent his son to the Moscow Conservatory to study. Tikhon took his first piano lessons from Kveton. Those were exciting and unforgettable sessions. Tikhon was a capable and diligent pupil who worked with a will. He was also insatiably inquisitive about all things to do with music. He showered his teacher with endless questions concerning piano technique and the theory of music. The boy wanted to know how and by what laws individual sounds were blended into melodies, how musical phrases were to be embroidered with variously colored harmonies, in short, how music capable of moving the hearts and of provoking thought, was created. "I was fortunate in that I had such a wonderful person for my first music master. I retain fond memories of Kveton who contributed so much to my early development as a musician," Tikhon Khrennikov would write half a century later. "As soon as I mastered the ABC of musical notation and learned to play the piano a little, I craved to compose on my own. It was an instinctive urge in me."

On the New Year's eve amid the lively general conversation at the height of a family party hardly anyone paid any attention to the eleven-year-old Tikhon who was hastily writing something on a sheet of paper in his lap, bending low over the table. "What are you writing, Tikhon?" someone asked. He made no reply being totally immersed in his work. Actually, he was writing down his first piano piece.

The following day he showed his étude to Vladimir Agarkov for criticism. An experienced musician, one of K. N. Igumnov's pupils at the Moscow Conservatoire, Agarkov had extensively travelled in the provinces. Having gained a reputation of sorts, he settled in Yelets where he

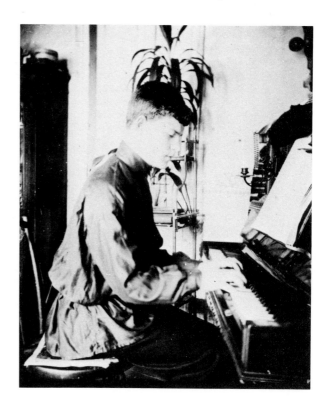

Tikhon Khrennikov with Dr. Mark Zilberquit, author of his first biography to be published in America.

made his living by giving private piano lessons. Those were the days of the *NEP* (Lenin's *New Economic Policy*) and most of his pupils came from well-to-do families. Agarkov charged a handsome fee, 25 rubles per lesson which was five times what other piano teachers in the town charged. The Khrennikovs could not afford Agarkov's lessons. But he agreed to give Tikhon an audition free of charge. As soon as Tikhon finished playing his exhibition piece, Agarkov said right away that he would give Tikhon piano lessons free.

The youthful author of that raw but carefully written piano étude was much inspired to hear a well-known teacher praise his first essays at composition. Apart from being a good pianist, Agarkov was also something of a composer who liked to show off his pieces at public concerts. Tikhon, who never missed any of these concerts, dreamt of following in his teacher's footsteps. Composing was an irresistible urge for Tikhon. Apart from piano etudes he also wrote marches, waltzes and, finally, romances. There was some no-nonsense and purposeful quality about the boy's appearance that made the audience suppress a smile and listen with polite attention. Mitrofan Khrennikov recalled that Tikhon did not particularly enjoy playing at the request of his home audience: even at that early stage he took composition very seriously. As he grew up his enthusiasm and industry seemed inexhaustible. Working tirelessly, with a rare sense of purpose, Tikhon was making good progress. The following two years proved decisive. In 1927 Agarkov left the town and Anna Vargunina took over as Tikhon's new piano teacher. This remarkable woman did perhaps more than anyone else to develop Tikhon's talent and mold his personality.

Anna Vargunina was more than a teacher for Tikhon. She was also a close friend. This remarkable woman had lived no less remarkable a life. Her stories about what she had gone through never failed to fascinate Tikhon. Born into the family of a wealthy factory owner, she graduated from a girls' college and embraced the noble ideas of bringing the light of education within the reach of the common folk. She made a clean break with her milieu and was out on a limb. In her student days Vargunina had lived for a spell with the family of Ivan Sechenov, an eminent Russian medical scientist. She frequented literary salons and concerts and generally tried to be in the mainstream of public life. Later she decided to devote herself to the education of children of the lower classes and took a teaching job in a remote village school.

When our future composer joined her class, Anna Vargunina was at a pretty advanced age. Seeing the keen enthusiasm and diligence of her gifted pupil, Vargunina was, herself, infected by his enthusiasm. Their lessons sometimes lasted for hours on end. She told Tikhon about the past, about the cultural life of Moscow and St. Petersburg, about art and literature. Vargunina had a good library made up of books by Pushkin, Gogol, Grigorovich, Danilevsky's historical novels and the biographies of great men. Tikhon's extensive reading widened his horizons and stimulated his interest in many different things. He was a good pupil at school where his favorite subjects were literature and history. He also did well in math (incidentally, mathematical ability ran in the family).

In the summer of 1927 Tikhon had another happy encounter which would largely determine his later life. That year a girl friend of Tikhon's sister visited with the Khrennikovs for a while.

She was Sofia Tseitlina, a student of Moscow's Gnesin College of Music. She once heard Tikhon play the piano and exclaimed: "He has real talent, I am telling you!" Back in Moscow she told Mikhail Fabianovich Gnesin about Tikhon. In the winter of the same year, when she revisited Yelets, she sent Gnesin the manuscripts of some of Tikhon's first compositions with a covering letter, an excerpt from which opens this chapter. Gnesin, a venerable composer and music educator, took an interest in the talented youngster. Two weeks later Tseitlina introduced her protegé to Maestro Gnesin in Moscow.

"On arrival in Moscow I showed Mikhail Fabianovich some of my first crude compositions. Asked if I should go into music professionally, Gnesin replied: 'It's hard to say at this stage what will become of you eventually. You have so much to learn about contemporary music and about the musical heritage of the past. Wide, profound knowledge is a must. You should concentrate on studying the work of composers of different centuries and countries ... Work hard, keep on learning and think. To learn to think well, young man, is all-important. This will help you make your final decision: whether you should go into music professionally or not. When you do, come back to Moscow.'

"The warm sincerity with which Gnesin received me produced a deep impression on me. Mikhail Fabianovich felt my gravitation towards vocal

Famed nineteenth century Russian poet Alexander Pushkin, one of the writers to whose works Khrennikov was introduced by his teacher Anna Vargunina.

music and presented me with a stack of sheet music containing songs of the classics of Russian and Soviet music."

Tikhon Khrennikov had a long association spanning many years with Gnesin. One of the founding fathers of the Soviet school of music and an experienced music teacher, he was the first to have discerned Khrennikov's talent. Gnesin kept in his archives the letters the gifted teenager from a small provincial town had written him long before he became his pupil. The first letter arrived soon after Khrennikov returned to his home town.

Dear Mikhail Fabianovich:

I owe you an apology for not writing earlier. I can't thank you enough for the wonderful sheet music you gave me and if I ever do anything worthwhile in music I will spare no effort to encourage and promote budding composers. That's a promise . . .

When I got back to Yelets I had an idea to write an opera based on Khomiakov's tragedy Demetrius the Impostor *and even began writing an aria for Marpha, the Tsarina (the lyrics are so beautiful). But I gave it up after noting down the first three lines of the monologue as the melody turned out to be too simple. Then I tried writing a sonata. I have completed the first part and am playing it now but it sounds different each time even though the themes are the same . . .*

I have to say "goodby" now. Once again thank you so much.

Sincerely yours,
Tikhon Khrennikov

Top: Mikhail Gnesin, a founding father of the Soviet school of music who discovered young Khrennikov's talent and was his teacher of composition at the Moscow Conservatory. Bottom: One of Tikhon Khrennikov's favorite composers, Modest Mussorgsky.

The letter showed its author's serious intentions and his urge of creativity. But it also showed that he was assailed by doubts. Should he embark on a professional career in music or not? He knew he had enough persistence and industry. But did he have enough talent? At the end of April 1929 Gnesin received another letter from Yelets.

Dear Mikhail Fabianovich:

It is over a year since I saw you. I hesitated afterwards to bother you with my letters as you are a very busy man. But now the time has come for me to ask you for advice on what are very important things for me. I decided to write to you again and send you my compositions. Do forgive me for trespassing on your time. In a month or so I will be leaving school. In the autumn I will have to decide what to do next. In June I'll be sixteen but no university will accept me because I am still under entrance age. My sister who lives in Moscow and Sofia Grigoryevna Tseitlina advise me to continue my music education. I love music more than anything else and I will never give it up but the question is whether I should go into it professionally or regard it as a sideline. I have to decide this question now. I confess I do not relish the prospect of ending up as a mediocre musician; there is no shortage of them, anyway. But to become a real musician one has to have real talent and that I doubt I have. I realize that it is difficult at this stage to say positively whether I will ever make a decent musician. At least I would like to know if my ability is above average.

I dream of continuing my music studies in Moscow where I will have better facilities. My sister has agreed to take me in. But if you

Composing was an irresistible urge for Tikhon—not yet sixteen years of age.

think my compositions are worthless I will have to abandon my dream and go to a village to work instead (school leavers here are given jobs in the countryside) and try and make my mark elsewhere. Mikhail Fabianovich, will you please reply to this letter and if you find time, do send me an assessment of my compositions.

I am sending the following piano pieces: Improvisation, *a* Waltz, *a* Russian Song, A Leaf from an Album, A Fantastic Dance, *and three romances:* An Old Jealous Husband, I Have Outlived My Desires, A Letter.

As I have done no theoretical subjects I am totally ignorant of theory, harmony, or counterpoint. I do not know the first thing about them. Looking through the music of romances recently I discovered that a romance should end in the same tonality with which it opens. But my romance An Old Jealous Husband *that I wrote in the summer of 1928 ends on a different tonality from the one it begins with. In my later romances I have tried to avoid this mistake. . . . And here is how I came to write the romance* A Letter. *A girl I know, who lives in Leningrad, sent me some score paper as a gift and instead of replying with an ordinary letter I sent her a letter with music. I think it is my best composition so far. My favorite composers are Mussorgsky and Rimsky-Korsakov. Apart from their romances I also like Rachmaninov's romance* Spring Floods. *The accompaniment is a piece in its own right. My most favorite book is Rimsky-Korsakov's* A Chronicle of My Life in Music.

**Ties of love bind Tikhon
Khrennikov to the natural beauty
of his homeland—the landscapes
he grew up with.**

. . . Should you advise me to continue my musical pursuits, do let me know if a knowledge of theory is a must for entering your college. If it is, I will work all through the summer on the course of theory you will recommend.

Mikhail Fabianovich, please write to me and answer all my questions. I want to know if my composing ability is progressing.

Do not send my compositions back to me, keep them. My sister urges me to continue my music education and asks you for advice on whether I should enter the Conservatory or your music college. I would prefer your college, but will I pass the entrance exams?

Respectfully yours,
Tikhon Khrennikov

The days passed but no reply from Moscow came. On June 7, after leaving school Tikhon sent a postcard to Gnesin which read:

. . . Here in Yelets I cannot fulfill my dream and so your reply is vital for me as I would come to Moscow, should it be positive, to take up music studies properly."

The long-awaited reply from Gnesin arrived the day Tikhon posted off his postcard. Gnesin was rather noncommital.

"One thing is certain: you have enough ability for you to become a professional musician. Therefore, you should come to Moscow and see me at our music college."

These words lent Tikhon wings. He left for Moscow with high hopes.

⋆   ⋆   ⋆

. . . The autumn of 1972. On the eve of celebrations to mark the 825th anniversary of Yelets, the municipal council conferred the freedom of the city on Tikhon Nikolayevich Khrennikov, the People's Artist of the USSR.

Many decades have elapsed since the day an ambitious teenager, unknown to fame, left his home town to enter the world of professional music. In this time Yelets lived through not a few momentous events. Yelets was one of the bastions which broke the terrible wave of the Nazi invasion in 1941. After the war the town healed its wounds and became bigger and even more beautiful. Throughout this period the composer kept in touch with his home town and its people. He visited it on repeated occasions in search of new inspiration.

The people of Yelets have been following closely the work of their famous fellow townsman. They are proud of his successes in music and in public life. Tikhon Khrennikov has always felt their support and attention.

I have lived my life in the full view of all of you, he said in a public address on one of his recent visits to Yelets. *And I only wish to be worthy of the trust and faith of my home town, and of my country, to bring people joy and to move their hearts.*

He lives a busy life and has the chance to revisit his home town only at long intervals. But each visit is a joyous and memorable occasion for him and for the people of Yelets. Khrennikov is very much aware of the debt he owes to his home town. *Yelets is my native town where I spent my childhood and youth. I went to school and had my first introduction to music. Here I knew the joy and excitement of my first public concerts at which I played my first compositions. In Yelets I experienced the first joys of youthful love and friendship.*

The Continuity of Traditions

The formative period in the career of a real artist is usually a long, complex and often contradictory process. Khrennikov's evolution was different: he had independent views even in school and later at the Moscow Conservatoire where he studied under the expert guidance of Professor Vissarion Shebalin whose dedication to the classical traditions and the rich song and dance heritage of the Russian people he came to share fully. In fact, Khrennikov's original talent was nurtured by first Myaskovsky and later Shebalin.

Yevgeny Svetlanov

"I have been fortunate throughout my life to encounter people who were totally dedicated to the art of music. They all had a genius for transmitting their love of music to all those who associated with them. This was the case in Yelets and later in Moscow."

Initially, Gnesin placed him under the guidance of Yevgeny Golubev, one of the senior students who later gained prominence as composer and music teacher.

Khrennikov followed two disciplines—piano under Yefraim Gelman, and composition under Mikhail Gnesin himself. A most stimulating and friendly creative atmosphere reigned at the Gnesin college at the time, an atmosphere free of petty tutelage and rigid regimentation. While encouraging their pupils to explore new areas and to enlarge their horizons the teachers knew how to keep them safe from those "aberrations" and "deviations" which were not uncommon in that stormy period. While heated arguments raged on the musical scene and time-honored musical values were often challenged and at times even dethroned, the Gnesin College of Music remained a serene oasis, a haven. This is not to say that the college was insulated from the winds of change and new trends or that the latest discoveries were hidden from the students. Emphasis was placed on instilling a sense of artistic responsibility into the students based on the solid foundation of the realist tradition. This healthy climate was determined primarily by the ideas and principles of the renowned Gnesin family of musicians who had the courage of their convictions.

Tikhon Khrennikov recalls:

Yevgeny Svetlanov, Russian conductor of world renown.

"Mikhail Fabianovich was a teacher of rare talent. Although our first lessons inevitably dealt with the ABC of composition they were absorbingly interesting with no academic aridness or theoretical narrow-mindedness about them. Our assignments were always interesting and challenging, being designed to stimulate the composer's imagination. They were all of a high artistic standard. The thrust of Gnesin's teaching method was aimed at releasing the students' creative potential. To get his pupils to think in concrete artistic images Gnesin gave them assignments of a program character. He encouraged his pupils to extend their knowledge of the outside world while keeping their feet firmly on the ground and their hand on the pulse of contemporary life. Mikhail Fabianovich taught them the art of giving clear and precise expression to the dominant idea in a rich graphic idiom.

Gnesin accompanied his lessons with fascinating talks about music and musicians. He used to tell us about Rimsky-Korsakov, and about his years at the St. Petersburg Conservatory. His extremely informative and vivid stories about major events on the musical scene of the day helped us to develop a serious and reverential attitude towards the art of music, to our future profession.

In those days we young musicians were attached to the workmen's clubs of Moscow factories and plants and we wrote music specially intended for amateur talent companies and musical education study groups. We were very much in the mainstream of public life and knew the people for whom we wrote our compositions. Mikhail Fabianovich followed our work closely checking everything we wrote and helping us to polish our pieces to give them a real professional touch. He urged us to maintain close links with the life of the community, and to set ourselves specific goals so that our first works had relevance. By his own personal example of dedicated service in the temple of art and by his teaching method, Mikhail Fabianovich helped us to develop not only as professionals each in his own particular field, but also as creative composers ready for their encounter with the future, for active involvement in public affairs. And he considered it a misfortune when some of us forgot for

Tikhon Khrennikov as a Gnesin Music College student (1928/29) in Yefraim Gelman's class. Center, Yefraim Gelman.

whom they were creating music, whenever in the undue enthusiasm for experimentation some secluded themselves in the ivory tower of sterile academicism. This did not mean, however, that he wanted us to follow in the familiar and well-trodden rut of established tastes. Far from it. On the other hand, he never divorced his own quest for new ideas and approaches from time-honored classical traditions. Central to his teaching method was his desire to mold us not only into excellent musicians but into good patriots and citizens as well. By a display of personal example he never tired of instilling into us all a high sense of public spiritedness and civic duty."

Tikhon Khrennikov, composer and public man, absorbed fully the lofty principles of his teacher who was one of the architects of the Soviet school of music and whose own life symbolized the continuity of the traditions of Russian and Soviet art. During the three years of study at the Gnesin Music College Khrennikov went through an excellent professional school. He evolved from a teenager from a provincial backwater into a young intellectual, one of the new generation of Soviet intelligentsia.

His first compositions bore the unmistakable stamp of his individuality and temperament but they were still on the raw side—a vocalise for soprano voice with string quartet accompaniment, a sonata for violin and cello, two movements of a string quartet . . . His progress was so rapid that in 1932 Tikhon Khrennikov was accepted by the Moscow Conservatory as a second-year student.

At 19 I joined Shebalin's class. My teacher was a young thirty but his prestige was already generally acknowledged. It is difficult to say what it was about Vissarion Yakovlevich's teaching method that was the most appealing: his tolerance or his respect for the as yet immature personality of a budding composer or his witty exposure of his shortcomings, his individualized approach to each of his pupils, or his desire to transmit to them his own knowledge, expertise and artistic taste. Shebalin's love for his pupils was invariably exacting. He did not give any concessions to bad taste, however slight, mushy sentimentality or falling in with the current fashions. I remember him as a great musician who has profoundly influenced my entire career."

Khrennikov with Yelena Fabianovna Gnesina, sister of Mikhail Fabianovich, also an outstanding pedagogue and co-founder of the school, college and institute named after the Gnesins.

Khrennikov entered the Moscow Conservatory at a most propitious time in its history. The decree of the Central Committee of the Soviet Communist Party of April 23, 1932 ended a period marked by confusion, endless organizational restructuring, disputes and discussions, most of which hampered the normal course of studies. The Conservatory was young and its student body contained many talents. Apart from well-known, venerable teachers such as N. Ya. Myaskovsky, A. B. Goldenveizer, K. N. Izumnov, G. G. Neuhaus, S. N. Vasilenko, G. E. Konius, F. M. Blumenfeld and A. I. Yampolsky the Conservatory's faculty had a number of talented musicians who had risen to prominence in the years of Soviet government. Practically every new school year introduced new brilliant names: Aram Khachaturian, Yakov Flier, Yakov Zak, Vera Dulova . . . In the dynamic and busy life at the Conservatory Tikhon Khrennikov was very much in the fore. I. I. Martynov, the musicologist, recalled:

Khrennikov immediately attracted attention. He was much talked about at the Conservatory and his compositions invariably excited interest and were eagerly discussed by the students. Tikhon Khrennikov established a reputation for high professionalism while still at the Conservatory.

Renowned Moscow Conservatory teacher Alexander Goldenveizer.

An active and gregarious person, Khrennikov immediately found himself at the center of many new initiatives at the Conservatory both in the sphere of professional life and in public service activities. He was very communicative and showed a lively interest in every aspect of life at the Conservatory. He was a veritable human dynamo. But of course his primary concern was music. Sergei Tsenin, playwright and actor, who was later to become one of Khrennikov's co-authors, emphasized in his reminiscences that already at the Gnesin College of Music Khrennikov *displayed an endearing openness of soul, that priceless gift of comradeship. His optimism and cheerfulness earned him many friends and generally drew people to him.* During his years at the Moscow Conservatory the charm and magnetism of his personality and the rich world of his creative individuality became increasingly more apparent.

He matured during the years of the first five-year plans which saw exploits on the labor front performed by Soviet people as they put into effect bold ambitious plans and projects. It was a time of quests for new ideas, of high hopes and, inevitably, of certain setbacks and losses . . .

Many years have elapsed since then and even the composer himself looking back over the vista of his life will be hard put to reconstruct many things with anything approaching documentary accuracy. The "magnifying glass of time" magnifies some things and inevitably distorts some things.

Brilliant Soviet pianist Yakov Flier, graduate of the Moscow Conservatory.

We have been able to track down, in various archives, some of Khrennikov's letters dating from that period along with a small note book, one of many Tikhon Khrennikov had while studying at the Moscow Conservatory. The period covered is 1932 to 1933. These notes were never intended for the prying eyes of strangers and certainly not for publication. They were strictly personal notes. Today they enable us to form some idea of the inner world of a budding musician, as they describe the range of his intellectual interests.

The very first entry in that note book, dated August 15, 1932, opens with a quotation from Stendahl:

Tikhon Khrennikov (third right, upper row) as Moscow Conservatory student. Lower row (right to left): Aram Khatchaturian, future famous composer, and Tikhon Khrennikov's tutors Heinrich Litinsky, Nikolai Zhilayev, Nikolai Myaskovsky.

Paul Hindemith.

A genius always lives in the thick of people like a spark within flint. And it only takes the right combination of circumstances for that spark to spring forth from the lifeless stone . . . Details of form and plot, however artistic, do not of themselves constitute art any more than ideas, however brilliant, give a writer the right to claim the title of a genius. To become that one has to integrate one's range of views and outlook in a way that would embrace and coordinate the entire world of contemporary ideas and to subordinate them to a single dominant idea. I cannot conceive of art divorced from the social conditions surrounding the life of the people. It is from the people that art derives its strength . . .

To these words Khrennikov added this footnote:

This idea must always guide everyone who enters the world of true art: whether he be a writer, a composer or an artist.

Even at that formative period, Khrennikov's range of musical interests was very wide. His favorite composers were Tchaikovsky and Mussorgsky (Khrennikov rejected the nihilistic trends which were current on the Soviet musical scene at the time). Like many of his peers he followed with close interest the experimental work of Hindemith, Schoenberg and Berg. He also studied the scores of Stravinsky, Myaskovsky and Prokofiev. Bach was his idol. One of the notebooks contains these lines:

Bach's soul is the soul of a human colossus who sees the seamy side of human affairs and expresses them in the language of his great art. Bach's music is an exploration of the real world of man as it is with everything that is evil and good in it. By no means is it the music of one who is preoccupied with his own personal suffering and experiences, who regards himself as the

31

Poster for the February 12, 1934
concert of the Symphony
Orchestra performing the works
of Khrennikov, with the composer
himself as soloist.

hub of the universe. Until fairly recently Bach's music failed to find an adequate response among our musical public. And understandably so. The fact is that our musical intelligentsia has been tainted (since the dawn of the 20th Century) and is still tainted with extreme individualism. The advent of Scriabin was no accident nor is Scriabin's philosophy a fortuitous phenomenon. It was Scriabin who until recently dominated the tastes and emotional responses of our music lovers and professional musicians alike. It is only a few years since the Scriabin scales began to fall from their eyes. Only now are we beginning to see the contours of that highly-principled attitude to art which finds such vivid expression in Bach's amazingly inspiring patterns of counterpoint.

I do not doubt for a moment that the slogan "forward from Bach" (rather than "back to Bach") is the only correct slogan for us that will advance the art of music in the formal sense. We should proceed exclusively from that content, but, like any other art, music has its own specific language, which develops naturally both in step with the development of content and in spite of it. I believe that Bach could help us more than anybody else in developing our musical language. Needless to say, any attempt at imitation of the content of Bach's music would be ludicrous. The content of our music should be rooted in our Soviet reality . . .

Khrennikov was eagerly absorbing new information and trying to sort out his experiences and impressions of what he saw, heard and read about in the books, seeking to project his experiences into his life's calling — music.

The impinging of a wide range of impressions on his professional sphere, in Khrennikov's case, served to enlarge his horizons beyond the world of music. He wrote in a letter to a friend:

Khrennikov with conductor Konstantin Ivanov.

I have recently read Lyass's book about Soviet students. Much attention is given to the attitude of men to women as established on the evidence of interviews and replies to questionnaires. One finding surprised and disappointed me. Asked "What do you think of love?" fifty one percent of those polled replied that they did not recognize any love for a woman, seeing her only as an object capable of satisfying their physiological needs. Only 49 per cent of those interviewed accepted, with qualifications, some definitions of love. I am convinced that only love is the source of real poetry in our life. As I see it, love constitutes the primary and true content of art in general and of music in particular — love for one's sweetheart, love for one's mother, love for one's friend, love for one's country, etc. . And if the majority of our young men do not recognize love they cannot appreciate music and literature and, as a consequence, they feel no need to hear music or read books.

The majority of those polled confessed that they did not attend concerts and read few books, if at all. I often go to concerts and I see much the same faces among the audience. I never see college students among them. This year I have given a few concerts in a number of colleges and I noticed that the majority of my audience showed little interest in music. And yet these are the very people who in theory should form the bulk of our national audience. These are the people for whom we must work in the first instance. We must therefore launch a dynamic massive campaign of musical education for the benefit of our college students and young people in general, otherwise everything will collapse. Attention is now being focused on raising the cultural level of our students but so far this has only been done by spurts. This is not good enough. A major change for the better will require a sustained effort on a long-term basis. I am determined to develop my own ability and potential to the utmost and then plunge into public affairs (community) activities in precisely this direction.

Tikhon Khrennikov and his long-time friend, outstanding French composer Andre Jolivet.

Khrennikov with Kara Karaev.

Tikhon Khrennikov's fellow student B. Mokrousov.

Today when Tikhon Khrennikov's activities as a public man are well-known, these words sound prophetic. And yet they were first set down in a private letter.

Khrennikov's spiritual world evolved in step with the development of his talent. Besides music classes, his schedule included concerts, rehearsals, participation in various evening parties and debating sessions, performances and art shows. All this opened up new horizons and stimulated his creative imagination. At the end of his second year at the Conservatory, he dreamed of studying piano technique seriously under Heinrich Neuhaus, who was the idol of the young pianists at the time.

He joined Professor Neuhaus's piano class the following year. However he did not complete the full course as composition was claiming more and more of his time. Even so, the training he got from Neuhaus was quite solid and stood him in good stead through his career as those who have a chance to hear Khrennikov perform his own compositions will tell you.

In the meantime his studies in Shebalin's class followed their normal course. A rare, creative atmosphere, at once stimulating and relaxed reigned in Shebalin's class at the time. Together with Yu. Yatsevich and B. Mokorousov, Khrennikov was among the first graduates of Shebalin's class. Years later Shebalin wrote:

> *I was in excellent rapport with Khrennikov in class. His refreshing and outstanding talent was evidenced by his piano concerto and first symphony (his graduation thesis) as well as by his scintillating music for the play* Much Ado About Nothing *staged by the Vakhtangov Theatre. Khrennikov wrote this music as part of his class assignment at the Conservatory and he played it to me on several occasions.*

35

Shebalin's teaching method presupposed the establishment of friendly relations between teacher and pupil as opposed to old-style tutorship with its implied unquestioning submission to authority. Khrennikov recalls: *Shebalin's class included many students with widely varying tastes and creative inclinations. Each one was free to compose in his own way, following his bent, even though all pupils deferred to Shebalin and respected his work highly. He had a genius for adopting a sensitive personalized approach to each student. This helped him bring out the individuality of each of his pupils.*

Two other musicians influenced Khrennikov's evolution profoundly. Khrennikov was one of the favorite students of Professor Georgi Conus, a veteran member of the Conservatory's faculty and a highly cultured man. The other musician who guided Khrennikov in theory and polyphony throughout his stay at the Conservatory was Heinrich Litinsky, a brilliant young teacher who later groomed dozens of young composers to a high standard of professionalism.

Heinrich Litinsky recalls:

Among his age mates Khrennikov stood out for his remarkable combination of an outstanding musical talent and the endearing warmth and charm of his personality. These traits of his character manifested themselves both in his academic studies and his everyday conduct and that drew people to him. Tikhon's willingness to help others was proverbial. This made Tikhon Khrennikov a favorite not only with his age mates but with people of the older generation who knew him. Khrennikov has fully retained this pleasing trait, and is just as helpful and cooperative today as ever he was.

Khrennikov receiving guest Mikis Theodorakis at the House of the Composers' Union.

I began my classes with Khrennikov with what we call the strict, austere style. The rather rigid formative framework of this tough course tended to put off many students. Khrennikov went through the course with enviable ease and deep creative penetration. He was able to do so thanks to his astute musical thinking which is what this highly specific discipline demands.

Khrennikov's talents began to come increasingly into their own in the field of polyphonic composition. Evidence of this was, among other things, his four-part partita for a string concerto. The serious musical content of the partita, its compositionally interesting treatment and overall artistic standard were most impressive. Khrennikov presented the partita with total success at a competitive exam at the Moscow Conservatory. I recall Myaskovsky's ecstatic reaction and his high appraisal of the slow part of the partita, the most complex in terms of artistic structure—the invention on four different themes whose vivid thematism and masterly handling would have done credit to any older composer with considerable creative experience.

Apart from his polyphonic skill Khrennikov's overall creative potential developed organically as his work in a variety of genres showed.

I recall the dynamic evolution of various aspects of Khrennikov's musical language within the mainstream of his overall growth and development and his means of expression: In harmony, polyphony, architecture, etc. . As one analyzed these processes one was struck by Khrennikov's singlemindedness, and his undeflectable sense of purpose. The natural ease and smoothness of his evolution as an artist is attributable, above all, to the emotionally and ideologically sound "basis" from which Khrennikov developed into a major composer and a prominent public personality.

With Belgian conductor Fernand Quinet, guest of the Khrennikovs.

In 1936 Tikhon Khrennikov graduated from the Moscow Conservatory.

In 1939 his name was inscribed in gold letters on the marble board of honor beside the names of Aram Khachaturian, Yakov Flier, Konstantin Ivanov, Yelena Kruglikova . . .

In the early 1960's Tikhon Krennikov returned to his alma mater, this time as a teacher of composition. This was the fulfillment of the once naive dream of the gifted teenager from Yelets: *Should I ever achieve anything worthwhile in music I will spare no effort in promoting and encouraging budding composers.* Tikhon Khrennikov has kept his word. He has launched so many young talents on professional careers in music that we can now speak of Khrennikov's school of composition. Among the dozens of graduates of the Moscow Conservatory who studied under him are Tatyana Chudova, Vyacheslav Ovchinnikov, Igor Luchenok, Alexander Tchaikovsky, Valery Kikta, Irakly Gabeli, Vladimir Pikul and Yekaterina Kozhevnikova, to name but a few. Their styles and temperament are widely different but they have all borrowed from their teacher something of his attitude to life, of his desire to help other people as best he can. In this way Tikhon Khrennikov carries on the tradition of his teacher, Vissarion Shebalin. Following are the impressions of Khrennikov, the teacher, shared by some of his former pupils.

Tatyana Chudova. Once in 1964 I showed him my first compositions for criticism. He looked through them and said: *"Tanya, why don't you play us the composition you yourself like best?"* I played the choir *April* and on the basis of that Khrennikov formed an idea of my potential and inclinations. This is just one example of the easy and friendly approach by which he establishes contact with a new pupil. Khrennikov has complete mutual understanding with each of his students. He criticizes or comments on our work in a tactful, well-meaning way. I think the primary principle of his teaching method is first to find the positive qualities in his pupil and only then look for shortcomings and their causes.

Distinguished orchestra conductor Konstantin Ivanov.

Student Tatyana Chudova plays one of her compositions while teacher Tikhon Khrennikov listens. "Khrennikov has complete mutual understanding with each of his students . . ."

Khrennikov with prominent Czechoslovakian composer Eugen Suchon.

What does he demand from us in the first place? Above all, vivid themes. Students often have difficulty in this respect. And he helps them to work out a clear-cut, vivid thematism.

But Tikhon Khrennikov also lays the emphasis on imagery. He is convinced that without emotions music is impossible, that music must directly affect the performer and, through him, the audience. Therefore he values the emotional content of thematic material. This does not mean, of course, that he pays less attention to form, or to the construction of a composition. He is very sensitive to form, being a supreme master of form himself. He spends a good deal of his time helping his students to develop a sense of form, using for the purpose, short pieces such as preludes, romances and songs.

I recall how once Tikhon Nikolayevich showed us the latest poem by Vsevolod Rozhdestvensky of Leningrad. Called *The Crimson Glow,* the poem was dedicated to Lenin. Our assignment was to set the poem to music. The choice of form was up to us. Khrennikov wanted to show us in practice how the same text could be interpreted in totally different ways and styles. A week later when we handed in our work there were ballads, poems and songs among them. A most interesting and exciting discussion followed. It was an unforgettable experience. It turned out that each one of us had his own idea of the possibilities of one and the same poetical text and interpreted its content in his own way. One wrote a composition in a placid epic style, another an impetuous and impassioned piece, still others submitted either compositions in grand style or, conversely, subdued and modest-sounding works. On that occasion we had a most interesting and heated discussion on the unity of music and the printed word, on how musical emotions lend new meanings to verse, how they disclose and amplify its message.

On another occasion Tikhon Nikolayevich suggested that we set to music Rasul Gamzatov's *The Land of Love*, a lyrical poem with a profound philosophical message. Once again we were free to follow our different ways in attaining a common goal which was to disclose the content of the poem: to convey one's love of one's native land, love for one's trade or profession, love for one's near and dear ones, in short, the full range of that profound and all-embracing notion "love" that the poem expressed so well. Many of us coped with the task reasonably well. In any case about half of the 15 versions composed on that occasion were later brought together in a collection devoted to Rasul Gamzatov. These are only some of the more memorable episodes that I can recall. I could go on indefinitely about the thorough way in which Tikhon Nikolayevich worked on our scores, about his attention to the problems of ensemble and to each genre individually. I could write a whole book about it. But I think the main thing about Tikhon Khrennikov, the teacher, is his broad interpretation of the work of a music teacher, an interpretation that embraces both the professional and the human dimensions. It often happens that after his graduation a student hardly ever sees his teacher. At best they may exchange congratulations on the occasion of some national holiday, or birthday. By contrast, all the members of my graduation class keep on coming back to the Conservatory to see Tikhon Nikolayevich and his class. Why? Because the Professor has never forgotten them, because he continues to help them in their work and in their creative pursuits. He introduces them to new performers, stage directors, ballet masters and promotes their compositions. In short, he does all he can to help his former pupils get on their feet. Needless to say, this is requited by a feeling of love and profound gratitude.

Alexander Tchaikovsky. Before joining Tikhon Khrennikov's class at the Moscow Conservatory I had studied piano under G. G. Neuhaus and later under L. N. Naumov. I hoped to become a concert pianist. I also secretly tried my hand at composition but those were only tentative attempts, of course, and even my parents were skeptical. Once I strained my hand playing the piano and had to give up piano practice for quite a while. It was then that I decided to ask Tikhon Nikolayevich his opinion of my potential as a pianist. His assessment was positive. Not only did he himself believe in my ability but he transmitted his confidence to me.

Tikhon Khrennikov is well-loved and respected by his students for his friendly and sensitive approach to all of them, as well as for his exacting attitude and honest criticism of their shortcomings.

We all know that Khrennikov is incredibly busy on account of his innumerable professional and public affairs commitments. Even when he goes on a short holiday out of town, which is not too often, unfortunately, he does not let that interfere with his schedule of teaching sessions at the Conservatory. But if for some valid reason teaching sessions *are* cancelled, Tikhon Nikolayevich will later give an extra lesson by way of compensation, either in his office at the Composer's Union or at home. Khrennikov's responsible attitude to his teaching responsibilities has earned him the respect of his pupils who admire his honesty and conscientiousness. It is also the mark of Khrennikov's supreme professionalism as a teacher, the mark of a real maestro.

His teaching methods are at once simple and complex. Tikhon Nikolayevich says that it is impossible to teach anyone musical composition nor is there any need to try to do so. What is important is to allow a gifted pupil to follow his bent, without petty tutelage and only adjust his progress by advice. Khrennikov allows the pupil maximum freedom in his quest for his individual style. At the same time he tries to guide his pupils towards creating good music for a discerning audience. He often says: *You are free to use whatever means you think are suitable for the achievement of your goal but never forget that your music should always be addressed to people.* He insists on this principle in his work as a composition teacher with his characteristic tact and an intelligent but exacting tutoring. This teaching method proved most effective.

One other distinguishing feature of Khrennikov's teaching method is what I might call his rejection of genre gradualism, which is typical of the approach of those music teachers who shepherd their pupils from the simple to the complex while keeping them dangling from strings, as it were. By contrast, Tikhon Nikolayevich adheres to a liberal approach. This helps the pupil to find his individual style more quickly and to take his bearings in the kaleidoscope of musical genres in a more relaxed atmosphere.

Soviet composers Tikhon Khrennikov and Andrei Eshpai with their Polish colleague Witold Lutoslawski and his wife.

A very special atmosphere marked by the maestro's close attention to each of his pupils, his benign attitude to them all reigns at Khrennikov's teaching sessions. Tikhon Nikolayevich even criticizes his pupils in a special way to avoid hurting their pride in the presence of their classmates. At the same time his criticisms are always fair and uncompromising. The pupil in this atmosphere thus does not lose confidence in his powers.

Boris Petrov. Although I entered the Conservatory as an aspiring pianist I had earlier tried my hand at composition while in the eleventh grade at Moscow's Central Music School. In the first year at the Conservatory I was fortunate to join Tikhon Nikolayevich's class. Once I showed my first piano trio to him for criticism. He commented without hesitation that I would do well to study composition seriously. Later Khrennikov enrolled me in his class. By then I had written my first compositions and even my earlier attendance at his lessons as a complimentary guest and my association with his students was a most rewarding experience.

What distinguishes Khrennikov's teaching method is his remarkable ability to stimulate his students' confidence in their own abilities and then to reinforce this self-confidence. Naturally, his pupils requite this attitude by love and affection for their teacher.

I recall one incident which occurred while I was still in the first year at the Conservatory. Though not knowledgeable of either polyphony or orchestration at the time, I told Khrennikov of my intention to write a piano concerto. He did not try to put me off by saying that I had everything to learn yet or that I was biting off more than I could chew, etc. On the contrary, he gave me every encouragement. It turned out, predictably enough, that my score was far from perfect, to put it mildly. And yet it was a very useful experience for me as I learned many new things while working on it.

Khrennikov always gives his pupils free rein to explore their own potential. He never imposes any hard and fast rules on anyone. What he does do is guide his pupils along with characteristic tact and subtlety to follow the best traditions of Russian and Soviet music. As students master the art of composition, creative quests and deviations are inevitable. Khrennikov never checks such wanderings and free exploration. He only adjusts a pupil's progress while preserving that which is most valuable, in his pupil's quest — the dominant idea, his musical thinking and individuality. Even the most daring and perhaps, controversial approaches and treatment of a theme never arouse his objections. What he does take exception to is lack of living thought, ideas and intonational expressiveness in compositions of his pupils. He likes to say that the theme of a musical work may be of any degree of complexity; what is not acceptable is lack of it.

While devoting a lot of his time to individual coaching Khrennikov sees to it that the rest of his class benefit as well. And they learn many useful things from his fascinating stories about his own work, his own experiences and those of other major musicians.

Spring

How did his idiosyncratic style take shape, a style that enables one to identify the composer of a work on the evidence of a single phrase? Above all this was the remarkable generosity of his melodic gift, the song-like basis of his language which runs through his works in any genre. And it is not merely a matter of the unique color and individual touch of his style of composing. Tikhon Khrennikov has introduced into the musical vocabulary his own particular intonation which is so unlike that of any other composer, his own harmonic turns of phrase, albeit somewhat unexpected, but always refreshing and very natural.

Yevgeny Svetlanov, the conductor

I hate talking much about my own experiences or confide in other people. What is happening in my inner world provides material for my future compositions. It seems to me that had I told others about my personal experiences I would never be able to compose music. There would have been no need for me to compose as I would have talked out the very things I wanted to say by means of my music (From a letter of August 1, 1934, Yelets).

The years of study at the Moscow Conservatory were packed with creative pursuits. Khrennikov displayed his rich inner world by means of music. Through his music he expressed his individual perception of the world and his attitude to it. It was this that made the compositions he wrote at the Conservatory so mature as to be easily superior to the common run-of-the-mill works of just another student, not only in terms of their intrinsic value but also in terms of his response to the passing scene.

On June 21, 1933 Tikhon Khrennikov made his debut as a composer and as a pianist. By his own admission he was "terribly excited" as his concerto contained passages with virtuoso-class technical difficulties for the performer. Khrennikov managed to overcome his pre-concert excitement and played his first composition dedicated to his teacher Vissarion Shebalin with great inspiration. However, his debut did not make much of an impact beyond the rather limited circle of the Conservatory's faculty and students. Among those who assessed his first concerto for its true worth was Nikolai Anosov who conducted the orchestra on that occasion. Anosov was a most discerning judge of music with a flair for new ideas. Shortly afterwards Anosov invited Khrennikov to join him on a concert tour in the city of Voronezh. There Khrennikov's composition was well received. In February 1934 Anosov played the concerto in Moscow on a program that also featured Mendelssohn's *Scottish Symphony,* fragments from U. Yatsevich's *Symphony* and Shostakovich's *Hamlet Suite.*

Later Khrennikov added a finale to his piano concerto. Interest in it among the conductors continued to grow. Noted conductors such as K. Saradjev, A. Melik-Pashayev and Georg Sebastian included it in their programs. It was broadcast on the radio several times. In those days "live" studio broadcasts were an important vehicle for popularizing new musical compositions as they turned the public spotlight on them.

Two performances of the concerto in 1935 decided its subsequent fortunes. On May 18 Khrennikov played it in the Grand Hall of the Moscow Conservatory. On that occasion he was supported by the All-Union Radio Symphony Orchestra under Georg Sebastian. In a rather ecstatic review A. Groman, the music critic of *Vechernyaya Moskva (Moscow Evening Standard)*, wrote: *"The most interesting of the compositions performed that evening was Khrennikov's piano concerto brilliantly played by the composer himself. Its appeal derives chiefly from its youthful energy and cheerfulness coupled with brilliant piano phrasing. The noted musicologist K. Kuznetsov in a brief reference to the symphony by K. Makarov-Rakitin which was also performed on that program, emphasizes, 'Khrennikov, a pupil of Professor Shebalin, follows a totally different stylistic line. Someone seated beside me whispered: "Here is the 'Moscow Shostakovich' for you!"* Indeed, Khrennikov has much in common with Shostakovich: the same urbanistic style, unlike that of Makarov-Rakitin and many other Moscow composers, whose output seems to have a strong rustic flavor being based on the themes and rhythms of folk music. Like Shostakovich, Khrennikov is both witty and observant leaning towards musical expressionism *and paradoxes. This is not to say that Khrennikov is in any sense under Shostakovich's influence. The two merely move in the same direction. The piano concerto is an excellent composition, both inspired and elegant, with an uncommon original piano style which is*

Khrennikov at a rehearsal of his First Piano Concerto. " . . . an excellent composition, both inspired and elegant, with an uncommon original piano style . . . What can be better than the composer himself playing the piano part with eclat!"

Conductor Alexander Melik-Pashayev, whose performance was one of the highlights of the Second International Festival of Arts in Leningrad.

Outstanding Soviet conductor Evgeny Mravinsky.

perhaps less effective in the orchestral accompaniment. What can be better than the composer himself playing the piano part with eclat! Georg Sebastian, the conductor, and each member of the orchestra, to speak nothing of the audience, were fired with a good deal of enthusiasm.

The concerto was included in the program of the Second International Festival of Arts in Leningrad. The Festival, a landmark event in Soviet cultural life, attracted the attention of many foreign musicians, music critics and ordinary music lovers. Among the festival's guests of honor were the outstanding pianist Leopold Godovsky; the Czech historian, musicologist and public figure, Zdenek Nejedly; Secretary of the International Theatrical Society, *Paul Gzell;* Director of the Warsaw Conservatory, E. Morawski, to name but a few prominent personalities. Interest focused on Meyerhold's sensational production of Tchaikovsky's classic *The Queen of Spades*, as well as on the superlative performances by V. Barsova, David Oistrakh, Melik-Pashayev and Eugene Mravinsky.

One of the highlights of the Leningrad Festival was the inaugural evening whose program, apart from classical staples by Glinka and Tchaikovsky, also included Khrennikov's *First Piano Concerto*, played by the composer. Khrennikov scored a triumphal success and had to play several encores. A *Moscow Daily News* correspondent who covered the Festival wrote that *The majority of the audience agreed that the composition of the youngest of the composers was the high point of the evening. The audience were particularly struck by the depth and maturity of the concerto's concept remarkable for a twenty-year-old composer.*

By the time the concerto received critical acclaim Khrennikov was fairly well known outside the Moscow Conservatory thanks to his first

A picture of Tikhon Khrennikov in later years.

essays in other genres. As early as November 1933 the first of a series of chamber concerts sponsored jointly by the Conservatory and the recently created Composer's Union were given in the Conservatory's Smaller Hall. On that occasion Khrennikov presented a cycle of five piano pieces dedicated to Anna Vargunina. Later Khrennikov unveiled his second piano cycles of three pieces. These were rather unpretentious straightforward concert miniatures, something in the nature of companions to his *First Piano Concerto*.

While the appearance of Khrennikov's piano pieces went relatively unnoticed, his first vocal compositions had a mixed reception. The critics and some of the Conservatory teachers for that matter accused them of a lack of lyrical sincerity and depth of feeling, imitativeness, and a banal piano texture. Khrennikov was not daunted by the challenge of competition from many recognized model compositions and proceeded to write three romances on classical Pushkin texts—*A Wintry Road* and *Don't Let me Hear Thee Sing, My Love* and *I Am Here Inesilya*. But performing artists including some well-known names: Vera Dukhovskaya, Knarik Grigoryan, Yelena Kruglikova, Alexander Alexeyev and Natalia Rozhdestvenskaya apparently thought differently and included Khrennikov's vocal works in their repertories.

Khrennikov's compositions were repeatedly performed during a national vocalist's competition in Leningrad. In particular Khrennikov's romance *A Wintry Road* found an admirable interpreter in A. Grigoryeva who emerged as one of the competition's winners. The newspaper *Soviet Art* later commented that the Leningrad competition ... *stimulated interest in vocal works by Soviet composers. . . . Already the Composers' Union has received requests for sheet music from leading singers for works by Shaporin, Zhivotov, Veisberg, Khrennikov, Levina and Dzerzhinsky.* This interest was a lasting one; Khrennikov's romances were often performed in 1939 as part of nationwide celebrations to mark the 140th birth anniversary of Pushkin.

But the attitude of the critics to these romances did not relent and so the label of "unsuccessfulness" stuck, quite unjustifiably.

During his last two years at the Moscow Conservatory Khrennikov concentrated on a new major scheme—a symphony. He started on it right after completing the incidental music to the play *Mick* by N. Shestakov written on a commission from the Moscow Children's Theatre. Khrennikov wrote at the time, *my work for the theater did me a world of good. Ever since then my overriding concern has been to make my music as expressive as possible. These days we encounter frequent cases, especially in the West, of a technical idea being allowed to dominate the content of a musical work. In this way the role of art is reduced to demonstration of a technical experiment, to musical gimmickry and contrivance devoid of substance. The great masters of the past took care to subordinate all of their inventions, technical devices and skill to the paramount goal of making their music as expressive and vivid as possible. We have to learn from them in this respect.* That was the credo of the young Khrennikov in his Conservatory days and this is what he still believes in today. Always has done, refusing to give in to the tempting considerations of the moment or the whims of the current fashion in music.

World-famous theatrical director Vsevolod Meyerhold, whose production of Tchaikovsky's *Queen of Spades* won great acclaim at the Second International Festival of Arts.

All in the family: Tikhon Khrennikov in his country house in 1937 with mother Varvara Vasilyevna and mother-in-law Yevgenia Vaks (standing on the porch), sister Sofiya and wife Clara (sitting), and brother-in-law Mikhail Vaks-Insarov (to the right of Khrennikov).

He composed the symphony in Moscow where he continued to live with his sister's family and where conditions of work were far from ideal.

For any graduate college student his graduation thesis is the climax of years of study. The graduation thesis summarizes the results of the student's years of study. It is also an indication of his potential and a foretaste of his future performance. Doubly so in the case of a graduate student of composition at a conservatory of music. The composition he submits to the examination board is judged, ultimately, not only by the examiners, who are specialists, but also by audiences, who are not. The examiners may well judge the graduate student's professional skill as excellent as a tribute to the knowledge and ability he displayed over the course of study at the Conservatory. But the "full marks" will give the young composer scant joy if his composition leaves the audience cold. If this happens, the first performance of a student's graduation thesis at the Conservatory may well become its last. This is what often happens, and it cannot be helped as real talent is a rare commodity. It is rare for a student's graduation thesis to remain in the concert hall repertoire. But that is exactly what happened to Tikhon Khrennikov's *First Symphony* his graduation thesis at the Moscow Conservatory.

Among those who immediately appreciated Khrennikov's talent was the well-known Hungarian conductor Georg Sebastian who lived in Moscow at the time. Sebastian decided to include the new composition in his repertoire and proceeded to work on it with enthusiasm. The names of the talented young composer and a popular conductor noted for his fiery temperament drew a full house at the Grand Hall of the Moscow

Conservatory on October 10, 1935. The evening's program was quite interesting and included, apart from Khrennikov's symphony, the French cellist Maurice Marechal with cello concertos by Honegger and Milhaud, plus Dvorak's *The New World Symphony.*

The first opening bars of Khrennikov's symphony took an immediate grip on the audience's attention. Once again they heard the highly original musical voice which they had liked so much when Khrennikov's piano concerto was presented. Once again the fresh breath of youth swept through the hall. The music was vividly expressive of the throbbing rhythm of our time, the spirit of the epoch . . .

My symphony does not follow any particular program. I merely wanted to express simple and ordinary feelings and emotions which accompany all of us in public and private life. Sorrow and joy, suffering and happiness—these are the theme and content of my music. It seems to me that the second and third movements are better than the first. It is they that express the creative faith which I have since professed. That was all Khrennikov had to say about his first symphony at the time.

Khrennikov with Dmitri Shostakovich. The works of the two composers were often compared by critics.

After the performance the audience and the orchestra gave Khrennikov a prolonged ovation. The following week the newspapers carried ecstatic reviews. Different critics found in the symphony not only merits but also youthful mistakes. But on one thing they were unanimous and that was that Khrennikov's symphony was a fresh and valuable contribution to Soviet music.

Interestingly, once again as six months earlier the critics again compared Khrennikov's new work with Shostakovich's music. At the time Shostakovich, of course, was the most prominent and interesting of the new generation of Soviet composers. While identifying elements of common ground in the work of the two composers the more discerning critics pointed to fundamental differences and Khrennikov's original world outlook and style.

M. Grinberg writing in *Soviet Art* stressed that a talented composer for all the influences he may be subject to always retains his individuality. He continued: *Tikhon Khrennikov on the evidence of his first symphony is doubtless such a composer. His music is noted for a specific quality peculiar to it alone. First of all, Khrennikov's symphony to a lesser extent than Shostakovich's music is subject to the influence of Western "modernistic" trends. Therefore the spirit of negation, rejection, the elements of sarcasm, irony and grotesque which are so strong in Shostakovich are much more muted in Khrennikov's music. For this reason this music is healthier, more naive and ingenuous. As compared with Shostakovich, Khrennikov's symphony has none of the grand scale which so overwhelms us in Shostakovich. Khrennikov seems to strive after a deeper message, after a more profound lyrical content of his music.* In a more detailed analysis of the symphony the critic wrote: *It should be noted that Khrennikov's symphony can be called a symphony by stretching the traditional sense of the term. The short first movement is almost totally devoid of the dramatic conflict that normally forms the nucleus of the first allegro of a usual symphony. The second movement is both original and interesting. Some of its turns of phrase and formal characteristics recall the famous* **Passacaglia** *from Shostakovich's* Katerina Izmailova (Lady Macbeth of the Mtsensk District). *But in terms of content and its implications Khrennikov's music is at the other pole. Whereas Shostakovich's* **Passacaglia** is expressive of deep suffering on a grand scale, Khrennikov's music is instilled with profound lyricism. This lyricism is free from subjectivist contrivance and whimsicality. Khrennikov's themes are rooted in the tradition of popular songs and this is the most salient and valuable feature of his music. At the same time the third movement betrays Khrennikov's youth and creative immaturity. At times the impression is that he has difficulty in controlling his material, that it tends to overwhelm him (a case of the tail wagging the dog?). Clearly Khrennikov has much to learn but even now it is fair to say that on the evidence of this symphony he shows excellent promise and that his music captures the spirit of our time well.

This assessment from **The Voice of the USSR:** *We have already said that in Khrennikov we have a major musical talent. His new composition—a symphony—is ample evidence for our judgment. The symphony has a distinct lyrical coloring. Written in a straightforward and colorful language, laconic and concise in format, the symphony has a strikingly powerful and sincere message. The symphony is dominated by a light and yet powerful energy and*

Arthur Honegger.

The younger generation: daughter Natasha with her son Andrei.

an irresistible will to live. Khrennikov's is a relaxed brand of lyricism but without any flaccidity or mushiness. Not only is it a talented and vivid composition but in many ways it is also a masterly work. Witness the organic construction of the second movement and of the finale, as well as the composer's complete mastery of counterpoint (without any flirtation with false virtuosity or a wish to parade his technique) and finally the brilliant, full-blooded and at the same time limpid orchestral texture of the symphony. (K. Sezhensky).

Sovetskaya Muzyka (Soviet Music Review): *The symphony's music is vivid, fresh, and graphically contrasting without being importune. It has a cheerful optimistic tenor despite the predominance of minor melancholic harmonies. Khrennikov's orchestral palette is interesting and vivid without being gaudy. (A. Drozdov).*

Vechernyaya Moskva (Moscow Evening Standard): *The symphony makes rather exacting demands on the composer. On the whole Khrennikov has emerged from this test with flying colors . . . The symphony, like his piano concerto, has a light and cheerful coloring. While the appeal of the concerto derived chiefly from its youthful spontaneity, in his first symphony Khrennikov displays a much greater measure of composer's maturity. The range of emotions covered is wider, too. The management of "light and shadow" is more confident and vivid as is, indeed, the interplay of moods. The symphony's dominant themes are also more expressive exhibiting greater skill in development, strength and completeness of form. (A. Groman).*

Finally this sketch from the newspaper **"Deutsche Central-Zeitung"**: *Tikhon Khrennikov is on stage facing an ecstatic audience giving him a standing ovation. The composer moved to emotion by his success, hugs and kisses Georg Sebastian the conductor. The scene is very moving: a young and highly gifted composer has just lived through the first public performance of the first symphony of his incipient career. He has just heard the Radio Symphony Orchestra under the baton of a talented conductor perform his symphony with rare inspiration and enthusiasm. He has also witnessed the tremendous success his composition has enjoyed with an appreciative and responsive audience. The symphony conveys well the spirit of socialist construction in full swing, the* *power of a brave new generation of Soviet people with their total faith in the future of their country. The symphony is a musical embodiment of our times. Nothing in the symphony is labored or studied, and everything has genuine quality and deep-felt emotion. (Bachauer).*

This unstinted praise was lavished on a twenty-two-year-old composer. He deserved every bit of it. Even those skeptical of verbal equivalents of music could hardly fail to see in this symphony a composite portrait of "the hero of the time". The joy of constructive endeavor, the purity and openness of lyrical emotions, deep thoughts—all this Khrennikov conveys well in his symphony. In fact, he was one of the first Soviet composers to have done so. It is important to emphasize that Khrennikov, unlike other Soviet composers, does not give a simplistic portrayal of his contemporary hero. The dramatic intonations of the symphony's second movement and, more specifically, the overwhelming surge of feeling of its climax is ample indication that his hero is no starry-eyed idealist.

*   *   *

A student of the Moscow Conservatory, unknown to fame, attained world caliber as a composer in a matter of months. A remarkable achievement by any standards. After its triumphal première in Moscow the symphony was performed in Kiev by an orchestra under Herman Adler, then in Kharkov under the baton of Alexander Klimov and later in other cities with equal success. Every subsequent season was followed by the composer's one-man concert appearances. His compositions were included in the programs of ten-day festivals of Soviet music and in the repertoires of many foremost performing artists. Newspapers and magazines carried profiles of the young composer. In the meantime he was busy polishing his technique as a post-graduate student at the Moscow Conservatory under the guidance of Vissarion Shebalin.

Great American composer Samuel Barber, a friend and correspondent of Tikhon Khrennikov since the mid-1930s.

Khrennikov's was, indeed, a meteoric rise to fame and not just in his home country but far beyond its borders, especially in the United States. In those days short-wave radio was a popular enthusiasm in America. Many Americans apparently had a particular pleasure in picking up on short wave music broadcasts from far-off Soviet Russia. Among other things they heard the live studio broadcasts of Khrennikov's compositions. Evidence of that was Khrennikov's abundant mail from his American admirers, professional musicians and ordinary music-lovers alike. Most of them liked his music; many asked for the sheet music of his works and wished the composer every success. The well-known pianist and music teacher Samuel Gorsky in a letter of October 20, 1935 wrote in his letter: *I have just listened to your playing from Moscow through the National Broadcasting System, and I enjoyed it very much. The reception was very clear. I am at present broadcasting a series of programs "Masterpieces in Piano Music" through station WDKC. If you would send me some of your compositions and permission to broadcast them, I would be pleased to play them on my program. I am sure my listeners would enjoy them as much as I enjoyed listening to them this morning.*

Here is another letter of the same date from pianist and teacher Tscharna Naschatier: *I would like to thank you for the colossal pleasure I had listening to your piano concerto. I listened to it with great interest at 9 a.m. on the radio. I would be very glad if you would tell me how I can get those other pieces which I think you have also written. I would like to play them at my next concert which is due at the end of January.* Khrennikov immediately obliged by sending her the music and at the beginning of the following year his piano pieces opus 5 were repeatedly performed by Naschatier and her pupils in New York. Since then they have been a prominent item in the repertoire of many music schools in Canada and the United States.

Among Khrennikov's American correspondents in those years was his contemporary Samuel Barber who later developed into one of the foremost twentieth-century composers. But in those days he was in the U.S. Army and in a letter to his Moscow colleague he not only expressed his admiration for his music but also complained to him that his superior officer forbade him to continue his piano practice off duty. In his reply Khrennikov mentioned that in the Red Army the situation was different: musical talents of Red Army men were being given every encouragment. That letter had an unexpected and most welcome effect: in his next letter Barber told Khrennikov that he had shown his letter to his commanding officer who at once gave him permission to have his piano practice. This marked the start of a friendship by correspondence between two young musicians.

Responding to requests from American listeners, the All-Union Radio Committee in Moscow organized a special concert on 22 March, 1936 made up of Khrennikov's compositions performed by an orchestra under Georg Sebastian. CBS broadcast the concert nationwide. But even before that concert *Musical America* and *Modern Music* carried extensive articles by Soviet musicologists V. Belyayev and G. Shnerson on the new wave in Soviet music. They focused on Khrennikov and Khachaturian. Finally during the 1936-1937 season American audiences heard Khrennikov's *First Symphony* in the interpretation of two of America's foremost conductors—Leopold Stokowski and Eugene Ormandy.

Those who gathered at the Musical Academy yesterday afternoon for Mr.

Tikhon Khrennikov greeting American composers (left to right: Roger Sessions, Ulysses Kay, Roy Harris) before a concert in the Moscow Tchaikovsky Hall. The Russian composer has many American admirers, both professional musicians and ordinary music lovers: evidence of that is the abundant mail he received from them.

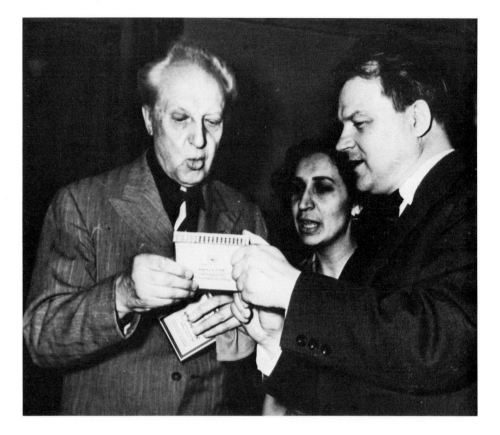

Khrennikov with American friend Leopold Stokowski, who was among the first to introduce Khrennikov's music to American audiences.

Stokowski's last appearance of the season were richly rewarded, wrote the Philadelphia newspaper **"Evening Bulletin"** on November 21, 1936. *They were justified in expecting a good performance but few of them could have foreseen a discovery of an exceptional talent on seeing the strange name of Tikhon Khrennikov in the program. The audience, however, felt that they were in for an unusual experience when Leopold Stokowski made a few introductory remarks and even asked the orchestra to play a couple of passages. This was clear indication that the conductor considered the composition worthy of special attention. And so it proved. By the middle of the first movement it was clear that the composer had an exceptional talent. It was remarkable that so young a composer should display such an original individuality of style, such confidence and skill in the handling of the big form. The symphony's appeal derives from its wealth of melody, and an ingenious approach. It is full of dynamism and expressive power. The orchestration is noted for its purity and remarkable originality. This may not be a fully mature work but the composer's creative individuality is in evidence from beginning to end.*

Other Philadelphia papers also carried favorable reviews with the critics calling the symphony *a work of considerable talent* (E. Schloss) and noting that *Khrennikov's composing style, simple, straightforward and sincere is in stark contrast to the affectation and artificiality, the pose and pomp of much of modern music. In fact, this is no modern music for someone who believes that the mark of the latter is atonality and technical gimmickry* . . . (L. Martin).

A Philadelphia newspaper quoted Stokowski as saying in his introductory remarks before the premiere *Everything has changed in Russia but the*

Russian character. Russian nature has remained the same . . . Summing up his impressions of the concerts in New York, Philadelphia and Cleveland the music critic of *Musical America* stressed that no other première during that season had been received by audiences with as much enthusiasm.

In February 1937 Khrennikov's symphony was repeatedly performed by the Philadelphia Orchestra under Eugene Ormandy. The New York performance of the symphony made a particularly great impact. The famous music critic W. Henderson in a detailed review published in the *New York Sun* wrote: Khrennikov's symphony *is without doubt the most promising work which has come out of Russia in recent years. This must be said with the music of Shostakovich still fresh in the memory.*

We could have quoted many more U.S. press reviews equally favorable to Khrennikov. But perhaps no less convincing evidence of the deep impression the symphony produced on American audiences was a fresh spate of letters U.S. music-lovers sent to its composer. Here are brief excerpts from just two of the letters apparently written right after the authors came away from the concert.

Talking to another welcome guest from the United States, composer Roger Sessions.

Tuesday, midnight.
Dear Mr. Khrennikov,

I have just returned from Carnegie Hall where the Philadelphia Orchestra under Eugene Ormandy played your symphony and I hasten to be among the first to congratulate you on this truly wonderful composition. It is almost incredible that you are so young. Your symphony is the best new composition I have heard in years. Truly it is a great achievement. Send me a photograph. Will you be good enough to autograph the enclosed program and return it to me? With my sincerest thanks for so much pleasure and to assure you that I shall eagerly await your future work.

Believe me, most sincerely
Arthur Vosper

Dear Mr. Khrennikov,

I trust you will forgive me this liberty I take in writing to you but hearing your Symphony *for the first time last night in New York City was a great pleasure and a distinct success. I am enclosing a review from the* New York Times *which will give you a good idea of how well it was received. I have read with great interest of your piano concerto and hope that someone will play it here in the near future, but how very much nicer it would be if you would visit America and give a complete program of your own compositions. I shall always look forward not only to hearing more of your music, but also to the time when you will come here . . .*

Sincerely,
Alfred Walter.

Tikhon Khrennikov with wife Clara and Aram Khachaturian, at one time his fellow student at the Moscow Conservatory.

Khrennikov's *First Symphony* continued to retain its appeal for American music-lovers. Since then it has repeatedly been performed in major cities all across the United States. At the height of the Second World War thousands of American music-lovers applauded Khrennikov's symphony when it was played in an open-air performance at New York's Lewisohn Stadium under the baton of Efrem Kurtz. Mark Schubart writing in the newspaper *Post Meridien* had this to say: *Like his compatriot, Shostakovich, Khrennikov isn't averse to the dry satiric touch. But neither is he scared off at the thought of writing a Tchaikowskian melody. Both are present in the symphony. It's an effective, tuneful and completely captivating piece . . .* Years later the Boston Symphony Orchestra under Charles Munch made a superlative recording of the *Symphony*.

It should be noted that Soviet musicologists of the post-war period failed to give a fair and discerning enough assessment (unlike the music critics of the 1930's) to these compositions. The attitude of the Soviet critical fraternity to them has been marked by a strange tendentiousness and even dogmatism. This is especially true of their attitude to the *Piano Concerto*. The impression is created that the critics have been seeking to perpetuate what we might call "their own exercise in wishful thinking." In other words to give their subjective assessment the status of an unassailable objective criterion. Unfortunately they have almost succeeded. According to them the *Piano Concerto* is allegedly full of assorted modernistic influences and is dominated by unduly sharp rhythms, a kind of "heavy-metal" mechanical stutter, abstracted 'play' of dynamic contrasts, rigid harmonies resulting from the linear movement of voices outside a clear melodic basis. Besides Khrennikov is also accused of being subject to various influences: in the first movement he allegedly imitates the early work of Stravinsky, in the second—Hindemith, in the third—young Prokofiev, and in the fourth—even Grieg. In short, while not denying that Khrennikov does exhibit signs of talent the critics usually present matters in such a way that the young Khrennikov fell under the spell of the Modernists, that he had ventured out on a totally wrong path.

Ironically enough, Khrennikov had himself to blame, up to a point. In 1935 he wrote: *The Piano Concerto was written when I was in my first year at the Moscow Conservatory. At that time I was a fan of Hindemith and Prokofiev. It is clear to us that the style of concerto writing followed by the romantics with its inevitable roulades, empty passages and elaborate piano figuration, etc., is no style for us in this day and age. We have to find our own attitude to the piano and our own piano style and texture that is economical, simple and at the same time brilliant, that could display the full range of the piano's phonic possibilities, the entire gamut of skillful pedalling. That is why while working on the* Concerto *I concentrated on purely technical ideas; and matters of texture were perhaps more important for me than music as such. As a result the music of some of the elements of the* Concerto *turned out to be less expressive, even abstract in musical terms.*

We should, of course, compliment the composer on his self-criticism. But we believe that the author's self-appraisal cannot be sufficient grounds for objective conclusions about the merits or demerits of his work. Besides, every major composer passes through several phases in his creative evolution. The composer analyzes them sifting the dross from the gold. Admittedly, the concerto did contain elements which Khrennikov later abandoned and never used again. But the main point is

Top: Igor Stravinsky. Bottom: Conductor Efrem Kurtz, whose performance of Khrennikov's *First Symphony* drew crowds at the height of World War II.

Alexander Gauk (top) and Gennady Rozhdestvensky (bottom), two of the best interpreters of the *First Symphony* in the USSR.

that Khrennikov was himself in that *Concerto*. It is hard not to see in this music both its profoundly Russian character, distinct melodic hard-core and purely Khrennikovian lyricism.

Here is the opinion of pianist Valery Kastelsky, one of the best interpreters of the Concerto: *The Concerto attracts me by its spontaneity, vivaciousness, youthful ardor and emotionality. It is a welcome challenge for the pianist. Although written by a very young composer, it shows a high level of musical thinking, skill and inspiration. You only have to hear the expansive, truly Russian breath of the second movement . . . Other examples include the whimsical grotesquerie, and cheerful scherzo in the third movement and the grand cadence in the finale with its blend of lyricism, humor and dance-like quality . . . To my mind this is perhaps the most spectacular finale in all of 20th-century piano literature. I am convinced that this remarkable composition, like Prokofiev's concertos, will continue to attract the attention of pianists.*

The *First Symphony* enjoyed even greater success. It has been played throughout the world. In the U.S.S.R. its better-known interpreters apart from the conductors we have already mentioned, include N. Golovanov and A. Gauk, V. Ferrero and E. Svetlanov, G. Rozhdestvensky and S. Turchak . . . True, even in the *Symphony* some of Khrennikov's detractors sought to find modernistic echoes while other critics were out to reduce the rich multi-faceted world of the *Symphony* to its lyrical, carefree mood and youthful spontaneity. In point of fact, however, the *First Symphony* contains pages full of high drama and these pages are no exception to the rule as his later work showed. Here is what Rodion Shchedrin had to say about it: *I listened to this music on many occasions and I was invariably impressed by its power, dynamism, sombre intense colors and the inexorable pressure of its rhythm. Together with Prokofiev's* Alexander Nevsky, *Shostakovich's* Fifth Symphony *and* Piano Quintet, *the* Violin Concerto *by Khachaturian and* The Battle of Kulikovo *by Shaporin, Khrennikov's* First Symphony *was one of the best examples of contemporary Soviet music on which many musicians of my generation have been brought up.*

The Composer and the Theatre

The composer writing music for a stage play is a creative contributor to its success or otherwise on a par with the playwright, director, stage designer and actor. The composer must become a close collaborator of the producer. His music cannot be viewed in isolation from the producer's overall concept, from the style of the entire production (1936).

The lure of the theatre had always been strong for Khrennikov. Perhaps it was the lingering effect of the plays he had seen as a child in his home town and especially of those stunning impressions of his first years in Moscow. Those were the days when the theatre was booming in the Soviet Union. Dramatists and directors vied with one another in daring and boldness as they sought to reflect the present and reinterpret the past. Their plays were the subject of heated public debate nationwide. Stanislavsky and Nemirovich-Danchenko, Meyerhold, Tairov and the younger generation represented by Zavadsky, Okhlopkov, Nataly Sats, those were the big names of the Soviet theatre . . . How could he resist being sucked into the orbit of these brilliant stars, into the exciting whirlpool of the theatre? Music in this whirlpool was given pride of place. The best composers often worked in tandem with the best theatre directors.

Leonid Polovinkin, a noted composer, who worked at the Musical Children's Theatre once introduced Tikhon Khrennikov to Nataly Sats, the theatre's director saying: *He is still a student. As a composer he may be too green but he has a divine spark, you know, individuality, and a fresh gift for melody. Why don't we try him? We run no risk and it should be a useful experience for him.*

What happened later is described well by Nataly Sats in her absorbing memoirs. Just then her Theatre was working on N. Shestakov's anti-Fascist play *Mick*. Nataly Sats decided to put the young composer through his paces in this particular play all the more so since there was plenty of time on hand and she could always backpedal if he did not cope. But her very first session with the young composer at the piano told her that she would not have to backpedal. She wrote: *I knew that it was bad pedagogics to heap praise on a budding composer but I could not help it as my joy eclipsed all other considerations. I knew that in him our theatre acquired a valuable young asset. We signed the contract right away and paid him an advance. For the next two months or so we met at the piano almost daily. He produced such vivid, tuneful and at the same time unexpectedly spectacular music that it stimulated me to keep on looking for new devices and ideas . . .*

Konstantin Stanislavsky, one of the greatest theatre directors of the twentieth century.

The happy father: Khrennikov takes a break from his busy public life in the company of daughter Natalie.

The boldness and originality of the 20-year-old composer who had never writ-
ten for the theatre before seemed incredible. I also admired what I thought
was the very Russian basis of his gift. He even looked very Russian, stocky,
of spare frame, with straight light brown hair, a stubby nose and a wonderful
smile which we did not see too often as he was usually intent on his own
thoughts. He was rather carelessly dressed with a bleak necktie always askew.
He was the darling of our company. We were all fascinated by his rich and
vivid imagination, creative individuality, his flair for style and form, and his
Russianness . . .

Inaugurating the Musical
Children's Theatre of Moscow
with art director Nataly Satz, on
whose request Khrennikov wrote
the music for the theatre's production of the anti-Fascist play
Mick.

Mick was first produced in May 1934. The reviews that appeared in
Moscow papers contained practically the first mention in the press of
Tikhon Khrennikov, well before the first public performance of his
Piano Concerto and the *Symphony*. K. Zelinsky wrote thus in *Pravda: The*
children's theatre has acquired a gifted composer of great promise. In the opi-
nion of *Trud (Trade Union paper) The tuneful music of the young composer*
Khrennikov is an excellent accompaniment to the play's action.

But the main thing was that *Mick's* music quickly caught on and was
included in the concert repertoire.

His first essay at writing for the theatre was thus both successful and
useful. Khrennikov said later: *The theatre is a concrete art calling for a con-*
crete attitude to it. My first work for the children's theatre helped me to feel
that creatively. He would return to a children's theme decades later but
from then on he maintained a permanent bond with the theatre.

Soon afterwards Khrennikov was commissioned to write music for yet
another stage play. This music brought him universal recognition.

It was one of those plays which leave a deep mark on theatrical history. This play was a new contribution to the development of the Soviet musical theatre.

We are referring to the Vakhtangov Theatre's production of Shakespeare's *Much Ado About Nothing.* What was it that made that production such a resounding success? First of all it was the remarkable harmony of all of its ingredients—I. Rapoport's masterly direction, V. Ryndin's imaginative stage design and the superlative acting by R. Simonov, Ts. Mansurov, D. Dorliyak, M. Derzhavin and A. Tutyshkin. But the motive force of the production, its prime mover was Khrennikov's inspired and innovative score. This score gave the theatrical community in the Soviet Union its first taste of a new type of theatrical entertainment—the musical.

The idea had been in the air for sometime. Progressive musicians in the West and in the Soviet Union, aware of the fossilized form of the old-style operetta, had been looking for a way out of the Procrustian bed of marionette-type characters and stereotyped situations. They wanted to find new forms of interaction between music, speech and movement while relying on the classical lyrical heritage, historical subjects and modern realist plays. This period produced such notable musicals as

Tikhon Khrennikov wrote more than one work intended primarily for audiences of children. Here he is shown with one very special little music lover: grandson Andrei.

61

Show Boat by Jerome Kern, *Of Thee I Sing* by George Gershwin, *The Threepenny Opera* and *Knickerbocker Holiday* by Kurt Weill.

Neither Rapoport nor Khrennikov had done any theoretical research but the goal they set themselves dictated its own means for attaining it. Rapoport told a meeting of the theatre's art council: *It is a musical play with songs, romances, dances and serenades. None of them is invented. As all have been integrated by Shakespeare into the play's action it behooves us to emphasize this dimension. Music is an integral component of the play and as such it has to carry its dominant lyric and comic lines.*

Khrennikov was very enthusiastic as he took up the challenge. After the production's premiere he said: *When working on* Much Ado About Nothing *my primary concern was to find common ground and a shared approach to the play with its director I. M. Rapoport which can only be achieved by friendly cooperation. To enhance the vividness of the play's characters, to reveal their substance and essence, the music must fully match the dramatist's overall design. The character of Shakespearean plays appeals to me and fits in with the thrust of my work. While working on* Much Ado About Nothing *I did not treat the play as a sort of museum piece, did not turn to the music of Shakespeaere's day rather, using contemporary means, I sought to express the deep-felt emotions, and life-asserting joviality of Shakespeare's characters. I also remembered all along that I had to observe a finely balanced sense of measure which is important for a composer writing for the theatre.*

It was accepted as a matter of course in those days that incidental music to any classical play simply had to have a period color. Khrennikov's innovative approach to Shakespeare lay precisely in the fact that he abandoned this principle and interpreted Shakespeare's heroes as live people of flesh and blood, as if they were his contemporaries. That is why his musical score has nothing that might recall either Italian Renaissance or Elizabethan England. Khrennikov freely uses the waltz, the gallop, the minuet and even a kind of polka— forms that simply did not exist in Shakespeare's day. On the other hand he did not try, as some critics alleged, to put Russian speech intonation into the mouths of the play's characters. Rather he gave them his own Khrennikovian intonation refracted in an interesting way through the emotional architecture of Shakespeare's comedy and that gave a unique charm to the entire score.

Khrennikov knew his Shakespeare pretty well even before the Vakhtangov Theatre commissioned him to write music for *Much Ado About Nothing*. And yet he decided against the period approach to the play. This throws a revealing light perhaps on the meaning of B. Asafiev's comment on Khrennikov's music for *Much Ado About Nothing* when he said: *The entire charm of this music derives from the fact that its composer came to the theatre, saw Shakespeare in his pristine purity and without doing any research on him, proceeded to write music for the play under the influence of direct impressions of what he saw. This approach is highly valued in painting: to see a chunk of life with a fresh eye as if it did not exist before. I think Khrennikov's talent has this quality and I dearly hope that he does not lose it.* Asafiev defined this quality as *the boldness of intonational simplicity.* All this was true enough but it would not have made Khrennikov's music for the play so enduringly popular had it not been full of beautiful and fresh melodies. They colored with their charm the lyricism, the humor and even the grotesquerie of Shakespeare's play. Soon after the production's first night Khrennikov's music caught on among the public. People sang it in the streets and in their homes rather like those tunes from the early operas of Verdi or the operettas of Johann Strauss.

But even authoritative critics who gave a high estimate to the Vakhtangov's theatre production and, in this context, to the composer's contribution to its success, could not pigeonhole its musical genre. Leon Feuchtwanger who saw it in early 1937 was more insightful for he emphasized: *The production's music and action are of a piece which is more than one can say about the music of* Othello *(in the Realistic Theatre) and of* Romeo and Juliet *(In the Revolution Theatre).* Sergei Prokofiev was among the first spectators of *Much Ado About Nothing.* Interviewed later by the theatre's in-house tabloid, he made a characteristically laconic comment: *The production is lively and fresh. Above all, Shakespeare comes across extraordinarily fresh in an easy and lively presentation: I am referring to the acting. The music is nice and the make-up, costumes and scenery are good.* Those who knew that Prokofiev was chary of praise realized that his *"music is nice"* meant a lot . . .

Work for the theatre was an important part of Tikhon Khrennikov's career, and he has many friends among famous theatre personalities—including ballerina Maya Plisetskaya, who is also the wife of his colleague Rodion Shchedrin.

After the success of *Much Ado About Nothing* Khrennikov was a household name in theatrical circles. He continued to cooperate with Vakhtangov Theatre. He also worked for the Central Children's Theatre, where he wrote music for E. Rostan's *The Romantics.* But there, of course, he faced a different set of tasks usual for drama theatre. A second chance to continue the line initiated by his work for *Much Ado About Nothing* presented itself five years later when the Vakhtangov Theatre staged Mikhail Bulgakov's *Don Quixote* (after Cervantes). *Don Quixote* brought together the same team of producers led by I. Rappoport, who did *Much Ado . . .* (only the scenery designer was a new face—P. Williams) and the same brilliant cast.

Don Quixote was even more of a musical play than *Much Ado About Nothing.* Serenades, songs, ballads, marches, and dances punctuated the action. Once again the audience watched a real musical which appeared long before Mitch Leigh's *The Man of La Mancha* and which was easily

superior to it in terms of melodic wealth. Rappoport, the producer, stressed that Bulgakov's play conveys well both the satirical and poetical musical color of Cervantes' novel. Significantly, Khrennikov while adhering to the basic principle of the integrity of the musical's dramaturgy took a different approach to selection of the thematic material, as compared to *Much Ado About Nothing*. In *Don Quixote* he left the local color of the novel basically intact. Even so the Spanishisms that peppered the score did not amount to stylization — the play was essentially modern in terms of its spirit and temperament. The production was dominated throughout by a balanced blend of lyricism and good humor, as well as by a healthy *joie de vivre*, enjoyment of life.

Khrennikov's tuneful melodies from *Don Quixote* had an immediate response from the audiences both in the theatre and on the concert stage. Later the composer brought them together in a light-part symphonic suite (of eight numbers).

He dedicated it to his wife Klara. *Don Quixote* was produced at the Vakhtangov Theatre on April 8, 1941, at the end of the season and was never presented again. The war intervened. After the war, unfortunately, this excellent paraphrase of Bulgakov's original play remained outside the attention of Soviet theatre directors.

. . . On October 4, 1942 in the city of Sverdlovsk, in the Urals, Moscow's Central Red Army Theatre company staged the heroic comedy *Long Ago* by the poet Alexander Gladkov. This romantic tale about the Patriotic War of 1812 against Napoleon was consonant with the sentiments and preoccupations of all Soviet people at the height of the Great Patriotic War against Nazi Germany. Consonant in terms of its patriotic

Tikhon Khrennikov with prima ballerina Galina Ulanova at the Barvikha Vacation Home near Moscow. This picture was taken on a skating rink (both the composer and the great ballerina are enthusiastic skating lovers).

message, optimism and faith in final victory. Its characters spoke poetry without any affectation in a strictly theatrical setting. Significantly, Boris Pasternak, the poet, in a discerning comment stressed the play's "charming ingenuousness of imagination". . .

The play was later produced almost simultaneously in different cities and its musical score was by a different composer in each case. The version that survived was the one written by Khrennikov for the Sverdlovsk production. Khrennikov was the only composer who was perceptive enough to convey the full measure of the "charming ingenuousness of imagination", and avoided the "petty stylization" Pasternak had cautioned against. And his music enhanced the play's patriotic message.

Today, forty years later, this musical is as popular as ever. Its record-breaking repertoire longevity is matched only by that of the Moscow Art Theatre's production of *The Blue Bird*. Without doubt *Long Ago* owes its enduring appeal largely to Khrennikov's excellent score.

Scanning the critical reviews of those days and the subsequent critical literature on this production, one cannot help wondering how the reviewers and other critics could have failed to miss the important discoveries Khrennikov made during his work for drama and musical theatres. To be fair, many flattering and even ecstatic compliments were paid to Khrennikov's handling of individual numbers of a particular score but they were all made in passing, as it were, and did not amount to an overall assessment. Fortunately it is not critics who, when all is said and done, determine the fortunes of a work of art.

As time went by the innovative essence and dramatic potential of Khrennikov's searchings were appreciated by leading theatre directors

Tikhon Khrennikov presenting a new composition to the actors of the Moscow Theatre of Musical Comedy.

who not only revivified the composer's earlier scores but in the 1960's persuaded Khrennikov to continue his work in this direction.

It was Eldar Ryazanov, an old-time admirer of Khrennikov's work since the days of *Much Ado About Nothing* who took the lead. He recalled later: *In 1944 I again had the pleasure of hearing Khrennikov's theatrical music in the Red Army Theatre's superlative production of* Long Ago. *In those days, of course, the Soviet forces were driving the Nazi troops out of the country, scoring victory after victory. Understandably the mood of the people was high and harmonized well with the production's optimism. Khrennikov's music, a totally organic component of the play, gave it a particularly joyous and lavish touch.*

As the years went by Ryazanov developed into a major film director and decided to make a screen version of *Long Ago*. To quote Ryazanov again: *I immediately found common ground with Tikhon Nikolayevich who accepted my overall concept — to make a film full of dynamism and joy. As I worked on the film's script I had to cut the original play quite a bit and consequently Khrennikov's musical score. And it was a wrench for me to edit each musical episode . . . I was determined to cut as little as possible as I loved Khrennikov's music so much and I often sacrificed the rules of the film game to preserve his music. I hope the audiences forgave me that. Khrennikov's music written for the stage production of* Long Ago *proved to be so multidimensional that it helped me to create an expressive and authentic period atmosphere in the film.* Ryazanov's film version of the original musical *Long Ago* was released under the title *A Hussar Ballad* and expanded the audience of Khrennikov's music to include millions. The success of the film was largely due to the fact that Ryazanov got his pitch absolutely right in exposing the organic links between the music and the spoken word which were inherent in the stage production.

Another director who appreciated Khrennikov's work was Vladimir Kandelaki, chief director of Moscow's Theatre of Musical Comedy. At the time operetta, once a very popular genre, was going through a period of deep crisis.

In the Moscow Theatre of Musical Comedy, after the first night of Khrennikov's ballet *Our Yard* and of Alessandro Casagrande's ballet *The Adventures of Pinocchio*. Second from left to right, Natalia Khrennikov, set designer; third left to right, producer Natalie Conus; to the left of Khrennikov, Casagrande's widow.

A scene from Tikhon Khrennikov's first operetta, *A Hundred Devils and One Girl*. Khrennikov boldly asserted his own ideas in the then declining, change-resistant genre of musical comedy.

As he looked for a way out of the crisis, Vladimir Kandelaki decided to invite to his theatre some of the leading lights of Soviet music: Kabalevsky, Shostakovich and Khrennikov, none of whom had any previous experience of working for the Theatre of Musical Comedy.

In the summer of 1960 while vacationing in the Crimea Khrennikov finished *A Hundred Devils and a Girl*, an atheistic operetta. The libretto, based on materials about the life of religious sects, was written by E. Shatunovsky. Kandelaki who produced it later recalled: *Undaunted by the 'prophets of doom' we decided to involve the audience in a serious discussion, punctuated by sketches offering pure clean fun while sustaining the atheistic message of the operetta. Our aim was to expose the hypocrisy and the essential dishonesty of those who exploited for financial gain the religious feelings of naive ordinary believers while covering up their unscrupulous machinations by the Gospel.*

The operetta went down well with the audiences and had a good press. The critics, with few exceptions, were unanimous that *each musical episode in the operetta is an integral link in the chain of its dramatic development* **(The Teatr Review).**

But even so, Khrennikov's first essay at operetta did not mark a significant milestone of his career. But then neither Shostakovich nor Kabalevsky were any more successful in their crack at operetta either. Unlike Shostakovich and Kabalevsky who never tried again, Khrennikov who was more persistent in asserting his ideas in this genre, which was so resistant to change, did.

While *A Hundred Devils and One Girl* was playing to full houses in Moscow, Khrennikov was working with E. Shatunovsky on a new

Scene from *A Hundred Devils and One Girl*. ". . . We decided to involve the audience in a serious discussion, punctuated by sketches offering pure musical fun while sustaining the atheistic message of the operetta."

Top: Scene from *Much Ado About
. . . Hearts,* a musical comedy
based on Shakespeare's *Much
Ado About Nothing.* Bottom:
Scene from *A White Night,* a
unique operetta that chronicles
the historic events of the 1917
Revolution in Russia. "No other
operetta before it had ever had
such a crowded cast . . . or as
heavy a concentration of events.
. . . This was Khrennikov's chance
to shine and he certainly rose to
the occasion."

operetta, *A White Night*, which he dedicated to the fiftieth anniversary of the Great October Socialist Revolution of 1917 in Russia. This work was to complete his trilogy on the subject of the Revolution: by then he had the operas *In Storm* and *Mother* to his credit.

Khrennikov's new operetta presented a broad picture of life in pre-revolutionary Russia "from the hovels to the palaces." The composer was aware that it would be impossible to squeeze momentous historic events into the traditional operetta format. To quote Khrennikov *The operetta's content dictated the form. Shatunovsky and I knew we simply could not do just another operetta in the traditional sense of the term. We had to find a new genre definition for the work. First we toyed with the idea of calling it a 'musical' but finally settled on "a musical chronicle" as being more fitting.*

G. Anisimov who produced the operetta in Moscow wrote at the time: *No other operetta before it had ever had such a crowded cast (more than forty characters) or as heavy a concentration of events—assassinations, transformations, the Emperor's banquets, the storming of the Peter and Paul Fortress, Kerensky's escape disguised as a woman . . . To adapt this play for the musical theatre it was necessary to find a special approach to its musical-dramatic treatment. This was Khrennikov's chance to shine and he certainly rose to the occasion.*

In the autumn of 1967 *White Nights* was produced in three different cities as far apart as Magadan (October), Sverdlovsk (7 November, producer V. Kurochkin) and Moscow (23 November). Later it was staged in other cities. One of the more interesting and successful productions of the operetta was staged at the end of 1967 in Sofia at the Stefan Makedonsky Theatre (producer Boris Pokrovsky, stage designers G. Kigel and N. Khrennikova). The Bulgarian musicologist V. Kristev commented: *In time it will attain a place in the history of operetta comparable to that of Pokrovsky's previous productions of Prokofiev's* War and Peace *and Mussorgsky's* The Khovansky Affair *in the history of opera.*

Six months later the Moscow Chamber Musical Theatre directed by B. Pokrovsky opened its first season with the comic opera *Much Ado About . . . Hearts* by Khrennikov and *Not Love Alone* by Rodion Shchedrin. The two are still running in this small but much-loved theatre (1983).

Pokrovsky has found a key which enabled him to give such a convincing interpretation to Khrennikov's music. *In Khrennikov's operettas musical numbers are milestones in terms of emotion and message linked together by spoken scenes into a single logical chain. I believe that this quality of Khrennikov's dramaturgy offers interesting possibilities to the director.*

Pokrovsky put his finger on it there. He has identified the dominant distinctive features of Khrennikov's approach to musical drama which fully apply not only to *A White Night* but to all the other works of this genre that preceded it.

The Right To Lyricism

I had long cherished the dream of writing a heroic opera about the history-making accomplishments of Soviet people. My attention was focused on the Civil War that followed the Socialist Revolution of 1917. But I was assailed by doubts that I would cope with a theme as grand as that. Until then I had chiefly worked in the medium of musical lyricism. After long reflections on the subject I concluded that our Soviet heroics and lyricism far from being mutually exclusive could be compatible in a vivid and fruitful blend.

The question of the musical language of the future opera settled, I needed a suitable plot. My final choice was N. Virta's novel Loneliness. *The action of the novel is limited to a small theatre of the Civil War—Antonov's mutiny in Tambov Gubernia. All characters are drawn from real life, Tambov peasant farmers. The triumphant march of the revolution is shown through their ordinary actions, reactions and attitudes . . . Tambov Gubernia, my native land, had long been known for its rich heritage of folk songs and I could draw on that.*

To begin working on the opera I needed a libretto. I had Virta's novel and the stage play Earth *based on it to start with. The librettists A. Falko and N. Virta had to contend with great difficulties. The novel showed the formation of revolutionary consciousness among the peasant masses. The task was to give as complete a characterization of the opera's heroes as possible on the basis of a severely reduced body of factual material as compared to the novel and the stage play.*

The abundance of song material introduced into the libretto provided the background against which I was going to build the opera's characters. That is why I leaned heavily on choral songs. The original libretto of In Storm, *which gave me a wealth of valuable material, had to be revised about a dozen times. It was particularly difficult to write music for that historic scene in the Kremlin when a group of Tambov peasants come to Lenin to learn the truth about the Revolution. In our treatment of this scene we swept all opera conventions aside. V. I. Nemirovich-Danchenko, the famous theatre director, contributed to the final version of the libretto by giving us valuable advice.*

We have already mentioned that lyrical music has a perfect right to a full-blooded existence in heroic opera. The question of major and minor forms should be decided by their intrinsic content, their ideological-musical and heroic meaning and significance whether they be arias, couplets or songs.

We deliberately rejected the leitmotiv technique as used by many of the world's foremost composers for the purpose. It seems to me that the leitmotiv method is justified when it either characterizes an idea as it does in Wagner, or is a purely illustrative element as in most of Rimsky-Korsakov's operas. The use of the leitmotiv for musical characterization of authentic, live people is fraught with the danger of "robotization" of the protagonists, of turning them into static figures and frozen masks.

The task was to "modify" my musical characterizations as the action of the opera progressed to show its characters in the process of continual development.

The problem of this kind of musical portrait painting, the search for vivid and easy-to-understand techniques of musical character delineation for the masses, the integration of the thoughts and feelings of all the characters in their common striving for truth, the legitimate and inevitable victory of the Revolution is the principal and difficult but creditable tasks that I set out to fulfill in my opera In Storm. *(10 August, 1938).*

The Revolution, with its romanticism and heroics, its turmoil and intrepid fighters, and the various ways in which it affected the personal lives of ordinary people and the destiny of their country had always attracted his attention. And as Khrennikov perfected his art and became ever more sure of his standing as a professional, he took more often a closer look at new revolutionary subjects and looked for books by contemporary Soviet writers on the subject of the Revolution that would be consonant with his own creative individuality.

Soviet composers on the Belomor-Baltiysky Canal construction site. Left to right: Tikhon Khrennikov, Nina Makarova (Mrs. Khachaturian), Nikolai Chemberdzhi, Vasili Nechayev, Vissarion Shebalin, Nikolai Miaskovsky, Victor Bely, Dmitri Kabalevsky, Aram Khachaturian, Vadim Kochetov and Klara Khrennikov (the composer's wife).

Top: Georgi Sviridov, one of the talented composers of Tikhon Khrennikov's generation. Bottom: Soviet composer Lev Knipper, author of the famous song *Field, My Field*, which was performed many times by Paul Robeson.

In this period digestion and portrayal of the Revolution and its implications and experience was the focus of attention of the Soviet literary and artistic community. *The Iron Torrent* by A. Serafimovich, and *Quiet Flows the Don* by Sholokhov, *The Debacle* by A. Fadeyev were followed by N. Ostrovsky's *How the Steel Was Tempered, The Optimistic Tragedy* by V. Vishnevsky, *The Wreck of the Squadron* by A. Korneichuk, *A White Sail Gleams* by V. Katayev, *The Ordeal* by Alexei Tolstoy. In films the release of *The Battleship Potyomkin* directed by Eisenstein was followed by E. Dzigan's *We are from Kronstadt, Chapayev* directed by the Vasilyev Brothers and *Lenin in October* by Mikhail Romm. In painting, the Revolution and its heroes were portrayed by K. Petrov-Vodkin, B. E. Ioganson, I. Brodsky, A. Deineka, and in sculpture by N. Andreyev, I. Shadr and S. Merkurov.

The Soviet musical theatre was lagging behind the other arts in this movement. True, the revolutionary songs of the early post-October years, Shostakovich's *Second Symphony,* Shebalin's *Lenin Symphony* and Knipper's *Fourth Symphony* were followed by a number of other musical works, but for a variety of reasons they did not make much of an impact. Only in 1935 was the first significant opera on the subject of the Revolution produced. It was *Quiet Flows the Don* by Dzerzhinsky which became a milestone in the history of Soviet opera. In his first press interview at the end of 1935 Khrennikov said that the younger generation of Soviet composers was facing the task of carrying on the successful beginning made by *Quiet Flows the Don* and producing good operas on Soviet themes. This ambition was shared by the more bold-thinking directors of musical theatres, above all those of Moscow and Leningrad. Conductor S. Samosud echoed this mood when he said: *Theatres need to work together with talented young composers. In particular we want to work closely with Khrennikov, Kabalevsky, Khachaturian, Solovyev-Sedoi, Sviridov and Khodja-Einatov.*

His meeting with V. I. Nemirovich-Danchenko, the celebrated director, was a turning point of Khrennikov's career. At the time Nemirovich-Danchenko directed both the Moscow Art Theatre and the Musical Theatre which bore his name. The great reformer of the theatre was enthusiastic about the idea of producing an opera on a contemporary theme. Nemirovich-Danchenko was convinced that his theatre, apart from the classics, needed a contemporary author writing on the burning issues of the day to satisfy the needs of the audience. For the Art Theatre, Anton Chekhov was at one time just such a writer.

That was how the paths of a venerable man of the theatre and of a young composer crossed. As Khrennikov recalls it: *One day I got a telephone call from Pavel Markov. On behalf of Nemirovich-Danchenko he asked me if I would be willing to write an opera for their theatre. I was stunned at the offer to work with Nemirovich-Danchenko himself. I could not believe my luck. I knew that Vladimir Ivanovich had attended the first public performance of my* Symphony *and was reportedly pleased with it. Needless to say I accepted the offer with profuse thanks.* A few days later Nemirovich-Danchenko called to say he would like a chat with me. He suggested dinner at the Metropol Restaurant. That was in the spring of 1936 just before he left Moscow for a holiday abroad. He wanted to discuss with me our future work before his departure. You can well imagine how excited I was. His magnetism was hypnotic. However my excitement passed quickly enough as I immediately felt that his interest in me was genuine. He suggested to me that I should sift through the latest Soviet novels for a suitable plot for a future opera. We agreed to meet again in the fall after his return.

In September, Nemirovich-Danchenko called me and suggested that I should immediately get hold of Nikolai Virta's latest novel *Loneliness*. As soon as I read it I knew that it was just what I had been looking for—a most suitable plot in every respect. My decision was probably also influenced by the fact that Virta's novel is set in Tambov Gubernia, my homeland. The novel describes the first post-revolutionary years, more specifically, the kulak rebellion led by Antonov which erupted not far from my home town of Yelets. Virta's novel was in many ways a recreation of what I myself had once lived through.

The novel had the right kind of dramatic tension and emotional intensity to inspire a composer. I told Nemirovich-Danchenko that I would work on the basis of *Loneliness*.

The choice was made but quests and problems were just beginning. Virta himself was too busy to write the libretto. Later he agreed to contribute to the text of the fifth scene—*Peasant Delegates Visit Lenin*. Khrennikov tried to interest Alexei Faiko in his project. He had first met him while writing music for Faiko's play *Alexander Shchigorin*. Faiko was a very popular dramatist who authored quite a few hits. And apparently the idea of wasting time on a rather thankless chore such as rewriting somebody else's novel into an opera libretto did not quite appeal to him. But Khrennikov proved to be a good persuader and Faiko eventually agreed.

I don't care a rap about Starokadomsky's opinion about Loneliness, wrote Khrennikov in a letter to Faiko. *I am re-reading the book and am sure that it can be made into an opera easily enough. The material is excellent and one only has to think about how to arrange it properly. The main thing here is to compress the events and so quite a few things will have to go out.*

When Khrennikov joined Faiko in Kalyazin they began to work together on the libretto and simultaneously on the score.

The long and painstaking work on the libretto involved Nemirovich-Danchenko's active participation. The composer and the librettist had regular discussions with the famous director. Nemirovich-Danchenko gave his younger colleagues a free rein and did not breathe down their necks even though he was an experienced dramatist himself. He was more concerned about something else. Khrennikov recalls: *He often spoke of the demands of the contemporary theatre such as realism, popular spirit, audience accessibility, depth of treatment and the laws of molding musical characters.*

The libretto and later the opera itself put the accent not so much on the damning indictment of the kulaks as on the establishment of a new way of life, on the irresistible march of the Revolution. The composer emphasized the social optimism of the opera. The lyrical line which he greatly amplified as compared to the novel fit in well with the opera's optimistic tenor. Long before the opera's première Khrennikov said: *While working on the libretto Faiko and I pushed to the foreground the lovers, Lyonka and Natasha, and the obstacles in their way. These obstacles were*

A scene from *Much Ado About . . . Hearts,* produced in 1968 in the Moscow Chamber Music Theatre and still running.

shown against a social and historical backdrop. In this way while developing the love theme we tried to recreate the historical atmosphere of those heroic years.

In January 1938 after a long tour the Musical Theatre company returned to Moscow and rehearsals began. Director E. Akulov who produced the opera recalled: *I remember the day well. Tikhon Khrennikov, our young composer, presented his opera to us with rare conviction and earnestness. His piano playing was impeccable and he performed the vocal parts with deep feeling . . . Even the parts for female voice, which normally sound somewhat comic when sung by a man, did not jar on the ear as Khrennikov's voice had a delicate quality to it. I had no difficulty in visualizing how it would all sound in the eventual stage version . . . I felt an impatience to go ahead with it right away . . .*

Originally the opera was to be premièred in the autumn. But the various alterations and final polishing delayed it by almost a year. It was only in April 1938 that Faiko submitted the final variant of the libretto in which many scenes had been modified and others made anew. As a result Khrennikov had to write quite a bit of extra music. Khrennikov invariably followed the advice of Nemirovich-Danchenko. He warned him and, indeed, other composers, according to P. Markov, *"against converting a dramatic work into a music drama by simply tacking on to it a musical score as often happened in opera. This kind of crude, mechanical adaptation to music compromises the dramatist's idea and concept."*

In 1937 Khrennikov presented selected excerpts from the opera's score at a national composers' conference and they received a favorable press. I. Martynov writing about the as-yet unproduced opera in *Sovetskaya Muzyka Review* described it as a major achievement: *The deep dramatic quality, organic theatricality and "stageability" of Khrennikov's music is certainly an asset of the opera.* N. Chemberdzhi was more reserved. He liked the opera on the whole for its sincerity and temperament but found in it elements of oversimplification and undue imitation without specifying, however, just whom Khrennikov was imitating. Early in 1938 a collection of selected excerpts from the opera was published and it immediately drew the attention of many singers.

It was not until the 1938-39 season that really intensive work on the opera's production began in earnest under Nemirovich-Danchenko's direction.

Nemirovich-Danchenko's prime concern was to subordinate to Khrennikov's music, in a harmonious blend, all of opera's theatrical elements to ensure an organic unity between the opera's musical action and its dramatic action, to represent truthfully and authentically human feelings and emotions on the stage of the musical theatre. To establish in opera the principles of a truly realistic theatre.

The theme of struggle for the people's happiness, for truth towards which the opera's heroes move following different paths, through a violent storm and trials, was the focus of attention of the opera's cast and producers led by Vladimir Ivanovich who defined the opera's dominant idea as the assertion of Lenin's Bolshevik truth.

This idea should permeate each episode, Nemirovich-Danchenko said. *Otherwise the opera runs the risk of generating a naturalistic piece of theatre. The audience, however they may enjoy the opera while it lasts, will come away without any significant impressions, largely unaffected by the opera's idea.*

Nemirovich-Danchenko conducted the rehearsals with great patience working at every scene and every character day after day for six solid months. He insisted that each actor and actress should identify themselves with their respective parts completely. He laid particular stress on the importance for each actor in rehearsal to think out carefully every detail of the actions and motivations of each character.

From the first Nemirovich-Danchenko urged the actors to play real living people, their contemporaries, to abandon the stilted operatic conventions and stereotypes. He said: *The art of our theatre has found its true vehicle in Soviet opera because this opera deals with the authentic and vivid sentiments and experiences of real people.*

In attaching prime importance to the musical side of the production Nemirovich-Danchenko in this context was perhaps more sensitive to the fourth scene which was the climax of the opera's lyrical line. He stressed that Khrennikov conveyed the entire dramatic meaning of the scene by a wide range of musical means.

Nemirovich-Danchenko considered the next (fifth) scene where, for the first time in Soviet operatic history Lenin, the leader of the Revolution, is introduced as the dramatic climax of the opera. He approached the character of Lenin from the standpoint of the composer's overall musical concept.

Nemirovich-Danchenko often said that the main task of the actor playing Lenin was not photographic copying of his mannerisms (although those who had known Lenin well commented that I. A. Petrov who appeared as Lenin did a remarkably realistic impersonation of the great leader); the main thing was to put the right meaning into Lenin's words during the conversation scene between Lenin and Frol Bayev, to stress Lenin's concern for the common folk. *This is the meaning of the scene. Everything here must have a deeper dimension. Because this scene epitomizes the message of the opera: peasants come to Lenin to be told the truth. It is as if the drama of all the preceding acts had become concentrated in this particular scene, in Lenin's office. You have to make the audience feel the significance of Lenin's words, to help them follow Lenin's thoughts and to recall the situation as it was in 1921. Tambov Gubernia, the local peasants deceived by Antonov and his kulak gang, and the vital need to wipe out the gang . . . Also to show Lenin's preoccupation with pressing affairs of state and at the same time his willingness to immediately receive the peasants in order to tell them the truth, to allay their fears and anxieties . . .*

Tikhon Khrennikov with conductor Boris Khaikin, working on the opera *Mother*.

The dress rehearsal, the result of three years of steady efforts, was held on the last day of the season, 31 May, 1939. The audience on that occasion was limited to professional musicians and the press. The opera's producers wanted to see what the audience response would be in order to make final adjustments. The dress rehearsal aroused a good deal of interest and press comment. The opera had its first night on 10 October, 1939.

Tikhon Khrennikov's new work went down very well. The opera played to full houses in the initial period. The composer and the actors had to take several curtain calls after each performance. The audience was captivated by the high drama and intensity of feeling, the lifelikeness and authenticity of the characters, the opera's revolutionary romanticism and the composer's innovative approach to a theme which was totally new for the opera theatre. Reinhold Glière, a distinguished master, called *In the Storm* one of the first successes scored by Soviet composers venturing out on a new path in tackling contemporary themes. G. Khubov writing in *Pravda* had this to say: *Khrennikov's vivid music shows great talent. The wealth of intonations, the range and variety of song-like themes that run all through the opera show that the young composer has a most admirable gift for melody. His harmonic language is crystal-clear and rich in vivid contrasts. Khrennikov's music is also noted for a lofty and passionate message, all of which makes the musical characterizations of the opera's heroes richer and full-blooded.*

Among the few attempts to reflect the revolutionary epoch in opera, Khrennikov's *In the Storm* stood out for the integrity of its artistic concept and treatment. The opera's persuasive power sprang above all from a harmonic blend of two strata—the social-historical and the personal-lyrical. In other words, the opera's characters were live people of flesh and blood, with straightforward musical characteristics, free from any grandiloquence, and placard propaganda. Khrennikov had succeeded in creating in his opera not only the period atmosphere but also typical human types and in this sense he was a worthy follower of the great realist tradition in opera exemplified by *Fidelio*, the early operas of Verdi, Glinka's *Ivan Susanin* and Puccini's *Tosca*.

The opera's music had a captivating melodic beauty. Khrennikov created his own idiosyncratic melodism on which he built the whole of the opera's score. Each act contained arias, ensembles and chorus noted for rare emotional intensity and charming song-like quality which delighted the audiences.

The opera was well received both by the audience and professional musicians. Among the latter was the well-known composer Isaac Dunayevsky who praised the new work in glowing terms: *The opera* In Storm *is an outstanding phenomena on the Soviet musical scene . . . The composer, using vivid and truthful musical colors, portrays the opera's characters well making the audience like some of them and hate the others . . . The opera moves the listener deeply. It is certainly a major victory for Tikhon Khrennikov.* Dunayevsky felt that the second and fourth scenes were superior in their musical quality to everything that had until then been done in Soviet opera. Dunayevsky also thought highly of those scenes which portrayed the people, especially the choruses in the third and sixth scenes as well as the musical portraits of the enemies. Of special

Composer Reinhold Gliere.

Famous classical composers Giuseppe Verdi and Mikhail Glinka (bottom, facing page) whose tradition of realism in opera Khrennikov followed in his work *In the Storm*.

Well-known composer Isaac Dunayevsky called Khrennikov's *In the Storm* "an outstanding phenomenon on the Soviet musical scene."

importance for understanding the subsequent fortunes of the opera was the following assessment given by Dunayevsky to the musical language chosen by Khrennikov: *Here Khrennikov shows himself not only as a talented composer but a bold innovator, as well . . . The range of his language is very wide, indeed: from the 'cruel romance' to symphonic generalizations, from popular country ditties to the most complex of vocal forms. Is it good or bad? In Khrennikov's case this is excellent, and is an asset. With youthful enthusiasm and boldness Khrennikov thinks nothing of using for his purposes 'cruel-romance' intonations, urban comic songs and ditties. In most cases he does so in the right place and at the right time and, most importantly, with great conviction. Songs dominate the opera whose composer uses them to express the most complex of feelings and emotions. This song-like quality of the opera is certainly one of its most valuable assets and its trademark.* It was significant that this particular aspect of the opera should have drawn such a flattering assessment from a composer who was a generally acknowledged master of song. And it was difficult to foresee at the time that this particular quality would trigger a storm of protest among the critics that buffeted the young composer so hard that his subsequent work would long be plagued by critical tendentiousness and lack of objectivity.

The first storm clouds on the critical horizon began to gather soon after the opera's première. On November 14, 1939, the newspaper *Sovetkoye Iskusstvo (Soviet Art)* stated that *the current controversy around T. Khrennikov's opera immediately went beyond the framework of a discussion of the opera itself acquiring fundamental importance in the context of the key problems being the Soviet art of opera.* This editorial introduced a selection of discussion items. Before long the debate began spilling over into the corridors of the Union of Soviet Composers.

Now, what were the "learned men" of the Soviet musical community arguing about during the very days when Khrennikov's opera was enjoying great success playing to full houses? The debate centered on matters of principle, on whether certain approaches to operatic treatment of certain themes was justified or not or, even to be allowed at all. Some critics accused the composer of violating the "time-honored, unshakeable" laws of the genre, of little short of demeaning, bastardizing opera by an intolerable turmoil of styles and a totally alien "low-grade" musical material. This inevitably reminded one of the abusive epithet "coachmen's music" that critics a century before flung in the face of Glinka, for his innovative music in *Ivan Susanin*. Khrennikov's "accusers" proceeded from laws and rules they themselves had laid down and judged the composer by them.

In the first place some of them denied the composer's right to lyricism claiming that the latter did not very well fit into the sweeping social-historical picture portrayed in the opera. One of the critics wrote: *Had Khrennikov written a simple lyrical opera about love or jealousy or some such subject our objections to his opera* In the Storm *would have been completely irrelevant. Instead he has produced, perhaps without realizing it, what we might call a popular musical tragedy and has composed it, rather incongruously, in the style of a sentimental melodrama.*

So, what should an opera be like? This is a question of definition, surely. And this question a critic cannot ask for; it is the composer's prerogative.

Another group of critics castigated the composer for an allegedly un-critical selection and improper use of thematic material. They categorically objected to the introduction into the opera of the intonations of urban song to the detriment of the rural song. Others complained about the presence of "cruel" romances which to them were a foreign body in the opera, inadequately enobled by the artistic genre. These criticisms were clearly didactic in purpose: the critics were trying to teach the composer just what kind of material he should choose for an opera. While the critics were concentrating their fire on things that were properly the province of the composer, they pretended not to notice the fundamentally innovative method used by Khrennikov in his opera: his free use of the song form to create full-scale opera characters.

The controversy heated up after the première of S. Prokofiev's opera *Semyon Kotko*. The two operas were closely related in theme and both dealt with the same revolutionary period. And yet they seemed to many diametrically opposed in terms of the artistic means they used as well as in fundamental structural features and thematic material. This led to sharp, but really gratuitous and unwarranted comparisons between the two works. *In Storm* was unconditionally defined as a "song-based" opera in which the genre-song forms predominate over the recitative-declamation development. *Semyon Kotko* was described as an exclusively anti-melodic recitative-based opera. The supporters of the two operas saw in them little more than an outline for the future development of the Soviet art of opera. One of the critics, A. Shaverdyan, subjected Khrennikov's opera to devastating criticism in an article that completed the press debate. While admitting that *In Storm* had enjoyed considerable success with the audiences and theatres he sought to prove that the opera won this success not thanks to Khrennikov's score but . . . in spite of it. He accused the composer of every mortal sin: primitive thematism, absence of true national character, disdain for the orchestra, etc. The critic was especially incensed at Khrennikov's treatment of the Lenin scene. After levelling heavy criticism at *Semyon Kotko* as well, A. Shaverdyan by way of summing up the opinion prevalent at the time claimed that *the works of Khrennikov and Prokofiev are polarized in terms of their stylistic trends.*

Great composer Sergei Prokofiev, whose opera *Semyon Kotko* was closely related in theme to Khrennikov's *In Storm*. Both works, written about the same time and often compared, stirred much controversy among critics.

It took decades for the critics to finally see the light: the two composers were following their different paths and both were making an innovative contribution to extending the range of forms and expressive means of opera. What is more, as the years went by it became clear that the quests of the two composers far from being polarized or incompatible exhibited more points in common in their approach to the themes and treatment of the opera genre than the critics, in the heat of academic polemics, could or cared to notice. But before the fog cleared both Khrennikov's and Prokofiev's operas were destined to be the target of not a few critical arrows.

Fortunately while the theorists were busy arguing various points back and forth, more and more theatres included Khrennikov's opera in their repertoires. So that by the beginning of 1940 the opera was produced outside of Moscow and Leningrad, in Saratov, Kiev and later in Kharkov, Kazan, Alma-Ata, Dnepropetrovsk and Kuibyshev.

★   ★   ★

At the end of 1952 the Stanislavsky and Nemirovich-Danchenko Theatre in Moscow announced its plans to produce a new author's version of *In Storm*.

The intervening ten years had seen a sharp downturn in the fortunes of the opera until its fairly early departure from the operatic scene under the hail of official arrows. The attempt made by P. Markov and P. Zlatogorov in the summer of 1943 to revive the Moscow production of the opera was unsuccessful. In 1946 the theatre was willing to stage the opera again but apparently the press had discouraged the enthusiasts. *Vechernyaya Moskva (Moscow Evening Standard)* wrote: *We feel we must warn the theatre and the composer that restoration of an old production without a radical revision of its libretto and musical material will only add to the old mistakes. True, some pages of this opera testify to Khrennikov's undeniable talent but one must not forget the grave ideological and artistic faults of the opera as a whole.* Yes, that is exactly how the paper put it: "ideological and artistic faults" . . .

In the meantime Khrennikov and his music had been becoming more popular, both in the concert hall and in movie theatres (Khrennikov wrote film music as well). His work became the subject of musicological research. Not only articles but whole monographs were devoted to the composer. The authors acknowledged Khrennikov's talent, praised him for his songs and admitted the merits of his opera. And yet one of the monographs that appeared in 1947 after a few flattering comments on *In Storm* continued: *What is lacking here is perhaps that which, above all else, should characterize Soviet opera, namely, artistic generalization of the vivid and intense emotions of the Soviet man of to-day.*

This seemed to complete the musicological assessment of the opera and it was not a particularly favorable one. It was then that Academician B. Asafiev, the leading authority on musical criticism, devoted to Khrennikov's opera quite a lot of space in his *Studies in Soviet Musical Creativity* which appeared in 1947. He wrote: *Tikhon Khrennikov's opera* In Storm *is the most talented example of that trend in Soviet opera which has commendably and justifiably sought to oppose direct perception, response, common sense and straightforwardness of human sentiments of the mass of listeners to their musical styles which are dominated by intellectualism for intellectualism's sake leaving too much in the art of music to logic and reason. It is my opinion that Khrennikov in his opera* In Storm *displayed a most welcome striving for simplicity in music, for a reflection of what we might call ethical directness of perception, in a much more refreshing, integral and immediate way than most of the other composers.* Asafiev rejected out of hand allegations that the opera was devoid of internal dramaturgy or that its musical material was static and heterogeneous. At the same time he was perhaps the first of Soviet musicologists who put the works of Khrennikov and Prokofiev in the same category, as phenomena of much the same order. He emphasized in particular: *Another valuable quality of the mass lyricism of Khrennikov's opera—is the lyricism of the simple-hearted peasant which the character of Frol epitomizes so well with his touchingly naive seeking after the truth which is an immemorial Russian tradition, and also in the muzhiks' chorus so full of the salty earthy peasant spirit, which celebrates the arrival of spring and the longing of the peasant soul after resuming peaceful farmer's toil after a long and forced interruption.*

If the irresistible charm of the realism of Russian art springs from simplicity, interpreted as the transformation of the humdrum and everyday routine and familiar mundane concerns, in short, the conversion of the truth of ordinary events and ordinary folk into beautiful simplicity and the simplicity of the beautiful, then Khrennikov on the evidence of his opera understood it well and felt it no less deeply than Dzerzhinsky did in his Quiet Flows the Don *or Prokofiev in* Semyon Kotko *and* War and Peace *since artistic embodiment of the simple truth of human affairs is a quality peculiar to the Russian people as a whole.*

Asafiev's favorable assessment encouraged Khrennikov who was completing his second opera *Frol Skobeyev* before returning to the score of *In Storm* for a fresh look. The experience he had gained in the intervening years enabled him to correct and adjust certain details. He also wrote a new overture and improved the orchestration. But in no sense did it amount to a radical revision.

The new production of the opera by P. Zlatogorov and N. Kemarskaya was most successful. Within the first season the opera was presented twenty-five times. The well-known critic E. Grosheva wrote: *Time is the best judge and time has proved Nemirovich-Danchenko right and the hostile*

Khrennikov with Academician Boris Asafiev, the leading authority on musical criticism, who esteemed Khrennikov's *In Storm* highly enough to compare the opera with the works of Prokofiev.

critics who made swinging attacks on the opera of our young composer which condemned it to a long period of oblivion, wrong. The new production of In Storm *put on by the Stanislavsky and Nemirovich-Danchenko Theatre, far from losing any of its freshness has increased audience interest and enjoyment.*

Subsequent developments showed that there was no need for any radical revamping to ensure the opera's repertoire longevity. It turned out that the creative boldness the composer displayed while working on the opera's original version proved sufficient to guarantee a successful future for it. The stage record of Khrennikov's opera has been extremely interesting and eventful, to say the least, over the three decades since it was first produced by Nemirovich-Danchenko Musical Theatre in Moscow. It can be safely said that no other Soviet opera has run for as long as Khrennikov's *In Storm* or in as many opera houses all across the U.S.S.R. Indeed, in the 1950's alone it played in Kharkov, Odessa, Perm, Sverdlovsk, Donetsk, Vilnius, Kazan, Tashkent, Gorky, Alma-Ata, Kuibyshev, Ulan-Ude, Novosibirsk and Ufa. Most of these productions stayed in the repertoire for years and many were repeatedly resumed. The opera has been produced abroad with notable success—in Dresden, Bratislava and Rusa.

We could have ended our story about a work that has now become a classic of Soviet opera on this cheerful, buoyant note but for one circumstance . . .

Ever since the debate that raged in the late 1930's around Khrennikov's opera the critics have quietly pinned the label of "song-like" opera on it. This "definition" eventually became something of a genre label, having migrated from critical reviews to the pages of musicological and music history works. Nobody knows how or why but this definition has acquired a distinct condescending connotation and having made the transition from a value judgment to a genre term, it began to imply something second-rate as compared to other "higher" species of opera. The term "song-like" opera has since been used by musicologists from force of habit, as it were, often quite out of context of the specific musical content of a given work. Another term "song-like dramaturgy" which is equally

Vladimir Nemirovich-Danchenko, theatre director of world renown, at a rehearsal of *In Storm* (Moscow, 1939).

vague and fuzzy has made its appearance as a derivative. Curiously enough, critics and musicologists have put into the category of "second-rate", in terms of genre, precisely those operas of Khrennikov and Prokofiev which they themselves in the not so distant past described as antipodal, polarized.

It would be useful at this point to recall the genesis of the term "song-based opera". It had its origins in the rich variety of popular musical presentations of the 18th century which in their essentially democratic spirit stood in opposition to the elitist theatre of the day. Song with all its genre and structural characteristics was the main and often the only "cell" of their music form. In the subsequent period song-based operas appeared in the West and in Russia. For all their democratic spirit they remained on the periphery of the opera genre even though they influenced traditional opera. The Soviet song-based operas of the 1930's performed a similar "democratizing" function and the merit of their creators was precisely the fact that they revitalized this long-standing tradition by addressing new song material characteristic of our revolutionary era, which catalyzed the opera of the day. We are witnessing a similar phenomenon in our own days. The proliferation in recent years of all sorts of pop- and rock-operas, etc., is indicative of a conscious desire to democratize the opera genre to influence it from outside at a new spiral of its evolution. Without attempting to assess their quality which must vary, we believe that this is yet another attempt at reviving "song-opera", a genre which while it does not, as a rule, leave behind anything of permanent artistic value does contribute to expanding the range of the expressive means of opera.

Wolfgang Amadeus Mozart (top) and Georges Bizet (bottom) used an abundance of song melodies as "building material" for their operas, as did Khrennikov.

We cannot, however, classify as belonging to this genre works which use an abundance of songs as "building material" transformed in accordance with the laws governing operatic dramaturgy. Otherwise we would have to put into the category of "song-based operas" quite a few operas including those of Mozart and young Verdi, Bizet's *Carmen* and Wagner's *The Mastersingers of Nuremberg*. This fully applies to the two operas of Khrennikov and Prokofiev, both of whom established the use of song as melodic material of contemporary opera. Herein lies their fundamental difference from the "opera-song writers" although the latter did exert a certain stimulating influence on them.

The attempts by certain critics to put outstanding Soviet operas into "closed" classification categories strike us as being so much musicological sophistry. This attitude is all the more erroneous in light of the fact that the character of these two operas and the methods of their composers (for all the differences of approach) were totally free of any dogmatism and one-sidedness. The entire diversity of today's art of opera as regards the variety of form, expressive means and techniques, strongly resists attempts at forcing living works into the straightjacket of traditional classification, which divides them into "melodic", "recitative-based", "song-based" etc., etc. The origins of this diversity are in the classics of Soviet opera: Shostakovich's *Katerina Izmailova (Lady Macbeth of the Mtsensk District)* and Prokofiev's *Semyon Kotko* and Tikhon Khrennikov's first opera *In Storm*.

The Hour of Courage

22 June 1941 turned the life of the country and my own life upside down. I did not fight on the battlefronts but like all my fellow countrymen during the war I lived for one thing only: 'Everything for the front, everything for victory'. I recall the tremendous inspiration with which we musicians performed to audiences of frontline troops, often in the aftermath of fierce fighting. We knew that the officers and men, weary with battle fatigue, needed our art as a morale booster for the battles lying ahead, wrote Tikhon Khrennikov recalling his experiences of the war years.

The composer moved into the 1940's bursting with energy and ideas and still largely youthful enthusiasm. And small wonder; he was not yet thirty. Invitations to perform in concerts and to give piano recitals descended on him from all sides. Since he showed great promise as composer and pianist, people expected much of him and he did his best to live up to their expectations.

April 1941: At the moment I am writing music for a new musical comedy film directed by Ivan Pyriev and written by Victor Gusev. This is my first major work for the cinema. I am planning to finish my Second Symphony *in the near future. It is in four movements. Ever since I finished my* First Symphony *in 1935, I have written no instrumental music to speak of and vocal music tends to "spoil" the composer. I also hope to start writing an opera on a libretto after Turgeniev. Turgeniev's plot fascinates me by its high poetry, musicality and the profoundly humane portrayal of human emotions. As I will be offering this opera to the Nemirovich-Danchenko Theatre, I intend to work on it in close cooperation with Nemirovich-Danchenko.*

June 22, 1941 came and played havoc with all his personal plans and long-cherished creative projects. The war delayed the realization of his immediate plans and made others simply irrelevant. Like all his fellow countrymen, he began to work frantically in a different direction. On the first day of war, Moscow composers met in emergency session at their cozy club in Miuss Street. The leading lights of Soviet music were there: Reinhold Gliere, Yuri Shaporin, Samuel Feinberg, Dimitri Kabalevski, Vano Muradeli, Victor Belyi, Lev Schwartz, Valentin Kurchinin, Matvei Blanter, Klimenti Korchmariev, Vladimir Vlasov, Vladimir Fere, Tikhon Khrennikov, and others. They came of their own accord, feeling an acute need to be together on the day a great patriotic war began. Gathered in the smallish auditorium of the Composers' House were the cream of the Soviet Union's musical community united by the spirit of friendly togetherness of like-minded people. It was a brief business-like meeting. The composers quickly agreed that they would all start to write mass songs for the army in the field. But they needed lyrics and lyrics were written by poets. Right after the meeting, a group of composers went straight to the Union of Writers. Had the composers been late by ten minutes or so, they would have had to receive a deputation of poets at their club. So it was that two streams met at the halfway point between their respective headquarters. Animated by a shared burst of patriotism, the composers and the poets immediately set to work.

Soviet composer Matvei Blanter, whose wartime patriotic song *Katyusha* has become famous all over the world.

That was the start of the unforgettable four-year long wartime tour of duty of the Soviet artistic community. Over forty songs were written within days of the outbreak of war. They were born of an incredible surge of inspiration that enveloped patriotic hearts and the best of them caught on immediately. They were sung by millions of Soviet people up and down the country. A reporter of the *Sovetskoye Isskustvo* newspaper wrote: *The Composers' House has been converted into a kind of song-writing assembly line. Some of the new songs are already being broadcast over the radio, others are being rehearsed by song and dance ensembles, by Utyosov's jazz band, the Philharmonic Society singers, and the Moscow Variety groups. The sheet music is on its way to concert organizations in the provinces. The State Music Publishing House is printing the best of the patriotic songs in huge editions.*

Needless to say, Tikhon Khrennikov was very much involved in this frenetic activity. The same reporter described the following episode: *Khrennikov arrived and showed his fellow composers poet Utkin's latest verse. "But aren't you going to set it to music yourself?" his colleagues asked. "So what? The verse is excellent and some of you may well write better music than I," the young composer replied.*

Today it is difficult to reconstruct the exact chronology of the fast-moving events of those grim days. But perhaps the first major wartime project completed by Khrennikov was to finish the musical score for the "peacetime" film called *The Swineherd and the Shepherd*. Director Ivan Pyriev edited in a strangely deserted, echoing Mosfilm studio after the evacuation following the first Nazi air raids over Moscow. Pyriev and his team were wondering rather anxiously how this carefree, cloudless film would be received by wartime audiences. It was then that the poet Victor Gusev added those famous lines to the lyrics of the final song written by Tikhon Khrennikov:

With world-famous pianist Emil Gilels in the days of World War II.

And when Nazi panzers come lumbering in. . .

That was how the war's sinister breath burst into an otherwise peaceful pre-war film giving it a totally discordant but topical tonality. Before the autumn was over, audience response showed that the film went very well. The newspaper *Sovetskoye Isskustvo* wrote: *The film* The Swineherd and the Shepherd *excited patriotic feelings in every Soviet heart, making us love our capital city even better, the whole of their country and all our fellow countrymen. The song at the end of the film is a stirring battlecry for the people to rise to the defense of their homeland".*

The tunes from the new film caught on immediately throughout the country to become a weapon in the life-and-death struggle against the Nazi enemy.

The well-known Soviet violinist Vladimir Spivakov recalls this episode relating to *The Song About Moscow* by Tikhon Khrennikov. It happened years later in Lvov during a concert tour in which Spivakov took part with Khrennikov. *Tikhon Nikolayevich was rehearsing a piece with the orchestra. A man called round and asked me to pass on to Khrennikov the sheet music he handed to me to get Khrennikov's autograph. He added that although he had never met Khrennikov before, his music had played an important part in his life. When the war broke out, he and his mother were evacuated. In the confusion resulting from frequent transport disruptions en route, the boy became detached from his group of evacuees. . .*

Violinist Vladimir Spivakov.

For the following ten days he rambled in the forest picking berries and mushrooms for food. Finally he was picked up by Soviet soliders from an artillery unit. They wanted to send him, like all evacuees, somewhere deep in the country's interior. But the boy refused to go. Instead he borrowed an accordion from one of the soldiers and began singing Khrennikov's "Song About Moscow" to his own accompaniment. The soldiers formed a circle around him and when he finished, they decided to let the boy stay as a son of the regiment. He went all through the war with the men of that artillery regiment. The boy made a contribution of sorts to the regiment's combat record. On the eve of offensive operations, the soldiers would set up a few loudspeakers and the boy would sing Khrennikov's songs over the amplifier system from a dugout. Nazi gunners would start shooting at the loudspeakers to shut them up. Soviet gunners would then get a fix on the Nazi guns and destroy them. So it was that in an indirect sort of way Khrennikov's music was something of a weapon on the front line.

Around that time another film was released. It was a totally different film, one of many that were made during the war. It was a film-concert entitled *We are Waiting for Your Return as Victors.* One of the songs in that film was written by Khrennikov to lyrics by F. Kravchenko. With its grim note and full of profound sincerity, it was an impassioned appeal to the officers and men of the Soviet army to fight the Nazi enemy to defend their homeland. And so many songs were devoted to that simple and eternally moving theme—a young soldier about to leave for the front says goodbye to his sweetheart. But only a few of those songs went down in the musical "Honors list" of the war. Khrennikov's *Farewell* was among them, thanks largely to the warmth and sincerity of its melody, its simple and restrained dramatic quality and also to its march-like rhythm that conveyed well the pulse of army life during the war.

The song was tremendously popular throughout the country.

In the autumn of 1942, Khrennikov joined his evacuated family in Sverdlovsk, the Urals... Here deep in the country's interior he continued to write music and appear in concerts in military hospitals, army units and at munitions plants. By then he was a household name wherever he went and was accorded a warm welcome.

At the beginning of 1942, Soviet newspapers carried two brief items, one of which announced that Tikhon Khrennikov along with the poet V. Gusev, film director I. Pyriev, cameraman V. Pavlov and film actress M. Ladynina had been awarded the Stalin prize for the film *The Swineherd and the Shepherd*. The other read: *Composer T. Khrennikov has recently written a march song for the Red Army, a new genre for him. The song has been approved by the Chief Military-Political Administration and will be printed in an edition of one million copies.* The item referred to the march-song *Everything for the Homeland*.

It seemed that songs of this nature were rather far from the composer's individuality and style. But Khrennikov proved flexible enough not only to retain his unmistakable style but also to inject a lyrical note into those songs to make them more dynamic and stirring.

Khrennikov also wrote a number of songs of a different kind which were just as popular. Among these was the song called *A Nice Little Town in the North*, a rollicking, comic song to words by V. Gusev. This song was put in the repertoire of almost every army song ensemble. Generally speaking, ever since their joint work on the film *The Swineherd and the Shepherd* Khrennikov and Gusev maintained fruitful cooperation and friendship. In the autumn of 1943, the two friends wrote a number of Komsomol songs. Unfortunately they were never finished as Gusev died. Khrennikov was to have yet another chance to use the lyrics left by his co-author when he wrote music for the film *At six p.m. After the War*. But more of that later...

Against this background it may come as a surprise perhaps to learn that Khrennikov also set to music several poems by Robert Burns as translated by Samuel Marshak. In point of fact, however, this change of pace was a perfectly natural development, the grim war-time situation notwithstanding. Khrennikov was particularly sensitive to poetry celebrating eternal human values, ordinary human emotions, precisely at his country's hour of trial in the crucible of war. The very spirit of Burns' poetry with its endearing folk lyricism and sincerity was akin to Khrennikov's kind of talent.

He selected five verses for his song cycle and wrote two songs for soprano, another two for tenor and one for baritone. Each song is a kind of small scene or a monologue. The vocal miniatures exhibit a variety of moods.

The Burns song cycle was performed soon afterwards on the concert platform, both in Sverdlovsk where they were written and later in Moscow. Their first performer was Yefrem Flax, a very popular vocalist, who sang them to the composer's accompaniment.

Khrennikov had first thought of writing his second symphony before the war. On the eve of the first night of the opera *In Storm* he told a newspaper interviewer: *At the moment I am working on my second symphony. Its theme—the heroic spirit of our days. At the same time it will be a lyric symphony. I hope to finish it by the winter.* His forecast proved too optimistic: he was distracted by his work on *Don Quixote* and later by *The Swineherd and the Shepherd*.

N.S. Golovanov, who conducted the first performance of Khrennikov's *Second Symphony*.

The first movement was completed by the start of the war. On August 2, 1941, it was broadcast over the air, performed by the All-Union Radio Symphony Orchestra under N.S. Golovanov. The symphony, according to one reviewer, was suggestive of a powerful dramatic force in it. They heard in the music not only the carefree mood of peacetime but also the distant rumblings of an advancing storm. . . In any case this is how the first movement sounds today to most listeners. Anything but a cloudless mood is suggested by the invocatory theme of the introduction and by the tense dramatic quality of the further development as well as by the uneasy, troubled reprise for all the light coloring and relaxed mobility of its concluding section. It is lyricism and heroic spirit in their contrasting juxtaposition that constitute the motive force of the symphony's dramatic development.

Khrennikov resumed work on the symphony after the Nazi invasion, early in 1942. By April, the second and third movements were ready and by the year's end, the symphony was completed. Needless to say, the war that had abruptly changed everybody's life, by the composer's own admission, dictated a new trend of his musical thinking. He wanted to celebrate the might and greatness of his country which would continue to stand steadfast as ever, having turned to ashes the forces of darkness that encroached on its happiness and freedom. He set out to convey by means of musical imagery the nation's irresistible will to win, to defeat the fascist enemy, to portray the staunchness and courage of young patriots.

The composer was understandably rather nervous on the day of the first public performance of the symphony on November 10, 1943 at the Columned Hall of the Trade Unions House. As he recalled it: *I realized that the people who gathered in the hall after a gruelling day's work at factories and plants or who had arrived for a brief stay in the capital from the battlefronts simply had a right to expect to hear something that would harmonize with that solemn spirit that informed their life and struggle in that great cause for which they battled sparing no effort, prepared to sacrifice their very lives.*

Both the symphony orchestra under the baton of N. Golovanov and the composer had a great success. Later the symphony was repeatedly

Pyotr Ilyich Tchaikovsky.

broadcast over the air and drew favorable listener comments. I. Nestiev, music critic of the *Moscow News*, the English-language newspaper, gave this penetrating assessment: *Perhaps the most significant event on Moscow's musical scene this month, outside of the production of Tchaikovsky's "Queen of Spades" at the Bolshoi was the first performance of the Second Symphony by Khrennikov... The symphony is the crowning achievement of Khrennikov's stylistic development in recent years... The first movement recalls the tense lyrical and dramatic themes of his pre-war opera "In Storm". The diversity and dynamic beauty of the popular crowd scenes in scherzo style bring back memories of those enchanting melodies he wrote for the Vachtangov Theatre's memorable productions. The first movement with its combination of traditional and juxtaposed dynamic images and the lyrical melody of the secondary part is particularly interesting as the composer builds Tchaikowskian episodes of exquisite emotional beauty introducing the somber and doleful recitative of the brass section. The expansive tunefulness of Russian folk music is admirably recreated by the poignant melancholy of the Andante with its delightful clarinet solo. The scherzo with its cheerful color, impulsive dancing rhythms and effective orchestration is perhaps the symphony's best section which ends in traditional style on a triumphant, stirring apotheosis.*

And yet the composer was not completely satisfied with the symphony's finale. *Something was missing, but I could not quite put my finger on it. I did a lot of thinking and analyzing before I realized that what was needed was another, new theme which would convey images of joyous merrymaking of young people, if still far off at the time. I wanted to express the optimism all of us felt even at the darkest periods of the war. I wanted to show that our people had inexhaustible reserves of optimism and faith, power and eternal youth. You can destroy just about everything that people make with their hands but you cannot destroy the forces of creation as such.* As a result, what was left of the original version of the finale was only its first theme — the elevated, lofty, march-like section that frames the whole of the concluding part. None of the traditional pomp that dominated the original version remained. Thus the entire concept of the symphony acquired an exceptional degree of dramatic integrity and logic of internal development. The musical narration is noted for a harmonious balance of the four components. Each of them performs its own semantic and figurative function. Neither the first movement (Allegro con Fuoco), as was once accepted in the classical scheme, nor the second — Adagio, as some musicologists seem to believe, can be properly called center of the symphony's dramatic design. If anything performs this function it is the finale. Linked to the finale is both the stern tragic tenor of the Adagio and the pulsating, throbbing rhythm of the third movement (Allegro molto) with its steadily mounting tension.

The *Second Symphony* is among the more spectacularly dramatic compositions of Tikhon Khrennikov. By his own admission, when working on the "war-time" sections of the symphony, he sought to portray in the second movement the sad and anxious time for the country, the victims of Fascism; in the third, to show the life-and-death struggle with the enemy — and to express in the fourth movement a feeling of coming victory and confidence in it. But it would appear that this rather literal interpretation of the symphony offered by certain musicologists on the strength of the composer's own sketchy account does not even begin to exhaust its rich multi-faceted imagery. In this respect it is the least reducible to a verbal interpretation among Khrennikov's other war-time scores. One thing is certain: in keeping with Khrennikov's highly individual gift it is not so much a "global optimistic tragedy" as a heartfelt and, ultimately, life-affirming lyrical drama. This feature of the symphony fully qualifies it to rank with the loftiest musical monuments of the Great Patriotic War which include Shostakovich's *Seventh* and *Eighth Symphonies,* Prokofiev's *Fifth* and Khachaturyan's *Second Symphony.*

The artillery salutes in Moscow marking the first Soviet victories in the war were still to be fired, the battle of Stalingrad was still to be fought and won when Khrennikov, in partnership with film director Ivan Pyriev and poet Victor Gusev, began work on a new musical film *At Six pm. After the War.* Khrennikov put his song writing experience, his diverse impressions of the war years and his unshakable faith in the final triumph of a righteous cause into the film's score.

The film was released in the autumn of 1944 and was widely seen as a kind of cinematic harbinger of victory. M. Ignatyeva, a Moscow journalist, recalled: *This film played to packed houses, and long lines for tickets formed outside movie theatres. We were all linked by the hope of an early victory in those days and to prolong the pleasure of indulging in our pet dream, we went to see the film again and again. The film certainly buoyed the people's spirit and helped them to live and fight through a difficult but great period.* What the audiences saw on the screen was not the director's fantasy but a desirable reality. It was not for nothing that after seeing that film, people established a sort of dating tradition of meeting at six p.m., like the film's characters, at the same old place, after the war. In 1944 the army newspaper *Krasnaya Zvezda (Red Star)* wrote: *The film's finale is deeply moving. . . The scene harmonizes well with our feelings today. This country is on the threshold of a great victory and as we look at the Red stars atop the towers of the Kremlin and the brilliant fireworks of victory salutes marking the end of the war we think to ourselves: "Yes, the day of victory is near!"*

Victory Day found Khrennikov in Berlin where he performed before audiences of victorious troops who had hoisted the flag of victory over the vanquished Reichstag. A few months before the war's end, he was sent on tour to the army in the field. That trip left an indelible imprint on his memory. Returning to Moscow he shared his impressions: *The winter of 1945 seemed to drag on and on. Early in March composer M. Blanter and I were leaving to take up our new postings with the Political Department of the First Byelo-russian Front Forces. It snowed heavily. At dusk the windows of all the houses in Moscow were blacked out and the curfew patrols were stopping the odd passerby still out in the streets after dusk. But victory was in the air, you could smell it.*

The breath of approaching victory was also felt in the air-splitting roar of Soviet guns firing at pointblank range at the last lair of the Nazi beast, and in the hurtling rush of the express train that carried us all the way from Moscow to Warsaw, capital of allied Poland. We reached the Polish-German border by car and stopped in a small hamlet. Here the Political Department of the Front granted our request to visit units of the legendary 62nd Army of the Guards commanded by Colonel-General Vasili Chuikov, twice Hero of the Soviet Union. We were to be received by the man who had commanded the

Aram Khachaturyan.

Tikhon Khrennikov in Berlin, in front of the remains of the Reichstag. (Far right: composer Matvei Blanter, who wrote the famous wartime song *Katyusha*). "It was in Germany that I felt with particular poignancy the greatness and indestructible power of my country and my people who had beaten into a pulp the hated Nazi enemy. The unconquerable might of my country was ringing and singing all around me in the heart of Germany."

victorious Soviet troops that had fought the advancing Nazi forces to a standstill in Stalingrad and then defeated them, and who later steamrolled the retreating Nazi forces all the way from the Volga to Berlin.

General Chuikov, his chest covered with an armor of campaign medals and orders, gave us a warm welcome and immediately invited us to dinner with members of his military council. Our first meeting with the commanders of the 62nd Army of the Guards lasted from 7 p.m. until 2 a.m. I don't know where they got the piano from but there it was standing in the corner, waiting.

Don't you think it's time for our dear guests to have their say! *Chuikov addressed us with a smile. From that moment on Blanter and I took turns at playing the piano and singing. Chuikov paid us an unexpected but flattering compliment:* I didn't realize that composers could sing their own songs so well. I would like, therefore, to give you my first combat mission: Go out to the boys and sing your songs for them. I guarantee a responsive and most grateful audience.

We spent the next two months in almost daily concerts for the officers and men of various units and services, and in hospitals. I particularly remember the concert we gave for the men of an artillery regiment who were the first to open fire on central Berlin. I sang my songs during lulls in the bombardment when the victorious symphony of Soviet guns died down only to resume with renewed fury shortly afterwards.

Once early in the morning when I finished my brief concert before the men of assault groups the commanding officer came up to me and presented me with his side arms. The men burst into hearty applause and I could feel my heart thumping with joyous excitement for I felt proud and happy beyond words.

It was in Germany that I felt with particular poignancy the greatness and indestructible power of my country and my people who had beaten into a pulp the hated Nazi enemy. The unconquerable might of my country was ringing and singing all around me in the heart of Germany.

...Three months later we returned to a Moscow flooded with warm brilliant sunshine by day and with festive lights by night as the capital gave a rousing welcome to the home-coming victorious troops. A few days after my return to Moscow I again met my friends, those gallant officers and men who now arrived in the nation's capital for the Victory Parade. We strolled the streets of Moscow and it seemed that the very air was filled with the wonderful breath of victory. My whole being was full of joy and pride that I was walking beside the men who had won this great victory for all of us, for their country and its people.

The Russian Figaro

While in Berlin during the days of victory celebrations I first thought of my lyrical opera Frol Skobeyev. *The opera's hero symbolizes the best traits of the Russian national character,* wrote Tikhon Khrennikov in 1946.

A different time called for different songs. . . Actually the idea of writing a comic opera had occupied Khrennikov since before the war. Back in 1939 he and Faiko discussed the idea of a comic opera on a contemporary theme: the everyday routine of life in the Red Army, and the attitude of young Soviet people to friendship and love. However, things did not get beyond the libretto.

Curiously enough, it was the critics who actually prompted Khrennikov to think of writing a comic opera. Many of them felt that he possessed the right kind of talent for this difficult genre. In February 1941 D. Zaslavsky wrote: *Our theatre-goers and music-lovers appreciate humor both in stage plays and in opera. Some of our young composers have a gift for comedy. Examples are many, including the* Scherzo *in Shostakovich's* Quintet *and Khrennikov's gentle humor in his delightful music for the Vakhtangov theatre production of Shakespeare's* Much Ado About Nothing *and yet no one has yet produced a comic opera.*

Later, even during the war, Khrennikov continued to cherish his dream. Various versions of the libretto were discussed. One dealt with a contemporary theme—Soviet student life. The composer had excellent co-authors in Lev Kassil and Victor Gusev. Who knows whether this idea might have come to realization but for the untimely death of Gusev? But all these years Khrennikov had been focusing on one dominant theme. And little wonder: the idea had been suggested to him by Nemirovich-Danchenko himself back in 1939, shortly after the first night of the opera *In Storm*. S. Tsenin, an actor turned dramatist, recalled: *One day on my way home I was walking down Glinishev Lane (now Nemirovich-Danchenko Street) when I met Vladimir Ivanovich out for a stroll. I greeted him and moved on when I heard Nemirovich-Danchenko calling after me. Whenever he met someone he knew he liked to have a chat. This time Vladimir Ivanovich told me that he wished someone would write a comic opera on the subject of the famous story* Frol Skobeyev *by an anonymous author. To my shame I could not say anything useful as I had clean forgotten what it was about. Vladimir Ivanovich then said that he knew an actor at the Maly Theatre who was very good at acting cranky old women and matchmakers.* Would you like to play a role like that? *he suddenly asked me. My heart sank and I could only blurt out:* Yes, of course!

A scene from *Frol Skobeyev*, Khrennikov's famous and much-loved comic opera about "a Russian Figaro."

Nemirovich-Danchenko then said that he knew only one composer capable of handling that kind of story, and that was Khrennikov: *He has a flair for a song-based treatment and a good nose for the really Russian in music. . .* Later I learned from P.A. Markov that Nemirovich-Danchenko had discussed the idea with him and with Khrennikov. His dream was a comic opera about a Russian Figaro which Skobeyev actually was. However the idea did not come to fruition as the war intervened. As soon as he returned to Moscow, Nemirovich-Danchenko called Khrennikov. The composer recalled: *During our separation Nemirovich-Danchenko had finally decided that I should write a comic opera based on* The Tale of the Russian Nobleman Frol Skobeyev *by an anonymous 18th-century author. This was made into a play last century by D. Averkiev and it had a successful run at drama theatres. Nemirovich-Danchenko said he was convinced that the material suited my individuality as a composer. He complained that too few national comic operas had been produced by Russian composers and he insisted that I should give this plot a good thought. I read both the original story and the play and little by little I warmed to the hero, a man of courage and intellect who never let his failures discourage him and who hated everything that was outmoded and moribund. Unfortunately Vladimir Ivanovich died soon afterwards and work in that direction somehow lost its momentum after his death. However, later I returned to the idea. My librettist was Sergei Tsenin.*

This was in the spring of 1943. Khrennikov was quite prolific during the war writing the *Second Symphony,* the *Burns Song Cycle,* music for a number of films and stage plays and many patriotic songs that became tremendously popular. So the composer must have been disappointed to read in the newspaper *Sovetskoye Iskusstvo* this unexpected and unfair reproach from M. Koval: *Tikhon Khrennikov, a talented operatic composer with a vivid individuality, has latterly abandoned opera and instead has been dissipating his energies writing variety and music hall ditties of, let us face it, rather doubtful musical quality. If there is anything of real value in Khrennikov's creative potential, it is his gift for lyrical and comic operas.*

This was written at a time when Khrennikov was completing the first act of *Frol Skobeyev*, a comic opera. In August it was ready. At the same time Khrennikov had finalized the opera's overall outline and character. He sought to infuse the new opera with a wealth of national color, vivid melodies and a dynamic *joie de vivre*. The diversity of comic situations and romantic collisions described in the original story coupled with its deep Russian coloring provided ample opportunities for that.

Khrennikov completed the final two scenes of the opera in the winter of 1946-1947 at a holiday hotel near Ivanovo. By autumn the rough draft of the score was ready and the rehearsals began shortly afterwards. Un-

Tikhon Khrennikov in 1947, the year he completed *Frol Skobeyev*—an opera that stirred much controversy among critics but enjoyed a tremendous success with the audiences.

fortunately, mishaps and mischances also began which would plague the opera's stage fortunes for quite some time.

Originally the opera was to have been produced by P. Markov and P. Zlatogorov who were later replaced by A. Popov and M. Kniebel, both theatre directors with no previous experience of work for the musical theatre. There was no unanimity among the critics and others about the very idea of producing the new opera. There were those who opined that Khrennikov's turning to events of the distant days of Russian history for a plot was premature and a mistake. These people strongly opposed the opera's production either at Moscow's Musical Theatre or anywhere.

Anticipating the objections of skeptics, Khrennikov defended his opera as follows: *The plot is relevant and close to the Soviet theatregoer of today by virtue of its vivid national Russian color, and the strong character of the hero. As I see him, the hero is a forerunner of the Soviet man of today with his adherence to high principle, an undeflectable sense of purpose, his* joie de vivre, *and his friendly and tolerant attitude. . .*

Samuel Samosud, the chief director of the theatre, was instrumental in producing the opera. Working closely with the conductor and directors were Boris Volkov, the gifted stage designer who had earlier done the scenery for Khrennikov's first opera and Aleksander Stepanov, a brilliant choir master. *Frol Skobeyev* was first performed on February 24, 1950. The cast was excellent. Among the soloists were those who had shared Khrennikov's philosophy and approach ever since the production of his opera *In Storm,* and younger actors and actresses. *That was one of the most exciting and colorful productions of my career,* recalled Larissa Avdeyeva, who appeared as Varvara. *It was a festive occasion for us all! I can think of only one other production that could match it in this respect and that is* Carmen *at the Bolshoi Theatre. We all looked forward to the next performance of Khrennikov's new opera. It was a real pleasure to sing in the opera which was making a tremendous impact on the Moscow musical community. This at a time when theatres were not terribly well attended. But* Frol Skoveyev *was one of the few productions which played to full houses.* G. Dudarev, another singer who was engaged for the first performances of the opera, wrote later: *I think* Frol Skobeyev *is the best of what Khrennikov has produced so far. . . After the first run-through at the theatre the opera captivated the future members of the cast with its exuberant diversity, wealth of melodies, graphic musical portraits, and the refreshing intonations of its language and tuneful recitatives. In it Khrennikov certainly displayed his intimate knowledge of the possibilities of every voice. That is why the lavish orchestration of the opera did not overshadow the singers.*

But the opera's subsequent fortunes were in many respects similar to those of Khrennikov's first opera. On the one hand, *Frol Skobeyev* was enjoying a tremendous success with the audiences who packed the house night after night, and on the other, there was the guarded attitude of the critics which on occasion developed into a biting criticism of the composer. A bitter controversy soon flared up which did much to contribute to the opera's early disappearance from the repertoire. Why? For an answer to this question we should briefly recap the opera's plot and describe its special features and characters. *Frol Skobeyev* is at once a typical and unique work. Typical in terms of the character of its plot; traditional both for the Russian and European theatre. It is essentially a

Samuel Samosud, the first producer of Khrennikov's *Frol Skobeyev*.

A scene from *Frol Skobeyev*. "As I see him, the hero is a fore-runner of the Soviet man of today with his adherence to high principle, an undeflectable sense of purpose, his *joie de vivre,* and his friendly and tolerant attitude . . ."

comedy with a familiar set of disguises, abductions, convoluted intrigues and at the same time rather naive conflicts and clashes which in the end are resolved in the happy weddings of two classical pairs of lovers—Frol and Anna, Savva and Varvara. Such plots are usually conventionalized and schematic to a certain extent. On the operatic stage, everything depends on the degree to which the composer succeeds in breathing new life into traditional situations and characters prescribed by the rules of the genre. Classical opera in this respect has provided many splendid masterpieces. Witness the immortal operas of Mozart and Rossini. . . And classical opera, for all its rather limited design, continued to feed the imagination of later composers right up to Richard Strauss. . .

The unique character of *Frol Skobeyev* lay in the fact that this opera was (and still is) the only musical embodiment of a picaresque comedy based on Russian national material. The critics could not of course have missed the profoundly national essence of the opera's plot and of its musical fabric as a whole. No one could have failed to notice the sumptuous vocal beauty of the solo parts, the duets and full-scale ensembles or the rare richness of the opera's symphonic palette both in separate orchestral episodes and in accompaniment. The audiences invariably enjoyed the enchanting lyrical episodes featuring Varvara and Savva in the second scene, Frol and Anna in the third, comic episodes involving Frol and Tugai-Rededin in the first scene, *Frol's Fortune Telling* in the third and the abduction scene in the fourth. The part of the hero, Frol, was brimful of *joie de vivre,* energy and temperament. The grotesque portrayal of the arrogant boyar Tugai-Rededin and the fussy old nuisance Mamka was full of generous satirical humor. The opera's dynamic action was organically sustained by a highly expressive, melodious recitative which retained the vividly national character of the principals' speech.

All this combined to produce a remarkably life-like musical and theatrical embodiment of the traditional precepts and characters of comic opera. And this held the unflagging attention of the audience which followed with bated breath the adventures and escapades of Frol Skobeyev, son of an impoverished nobleman who challenged the powers that be.

But the opera also had its imperfections which stemmed largely from flaws in its dramatic design; as a result, the opera's action was over-saturated with distracting detail and undue emphasis on the sociological aspect. However, it was not these drawbacks that came under fire. Reviewers attacked the opera from different angles. Some accused Khrennikov of a false recreation of the musical color of the period, of neglecting the folklore material. Others charged that the opera was over-saturated with recitative at the expense of vivid melodies (?!), that the composer abused modulation and harmonic complexities and so on and so forth. A minority of the critics were discerning enough to reject these and other charges giving strong reasons for their dissenting opinion. Still other critics charged that the composer and the librettist had sinned against historical truth and were allegedly apologizing for the mores of a bygone age. Finally, there were those who even denied Khrennikov's right to use this kind of plot at all. Echoing this strange point of view, the newspaper *Sovetskoye Isskustvo* editorialized: *It is a matter of regret that the composer, the librettist and the theatre's company have wasted so much effort and time to produce an opera crowded with characters belonging to a totally irrelevant past.*

Scenes from *Frol Skobeyev* (the title was later changed to The Low-born Son-in-Law), still the only musical embodiment of a picaresque comedy based on Russian national material. "The plot is relevant and close to the Soviet theatregoer of today by virtue of its vivid national Russian color, and the strong character of the hero."

However, this verdict was not supported by thousands of opera goers and music lovers who packed the house night after night and who later expressed their opinions of the opera in their letters to the editors of leading national dailies and news magazines. The newspaper *Sovetskoye Isskustvo* had to start a special column, *Theatregoers Speak*, which carried readers' comments on Khrennikov's opera. People from all walks of life — workers, students, scientists, servicemen, people prominent in the arts, etc., sent in their letters. This ready public response alone was evidence of the tremendous impact the opera had made. Naturally some of the letters were also critical, but the vast majority were favorable.

And yet despite this positive public response, the critics would not change their minds. While conceding some of the opera's musical merits, the critics passed a harsh and apparently final verdict on the opera. As V. Kukharski noted several years later, the opera was dubbed an ideological failure: *They demanded from the hero of an unpretentious comic opera nothing short of being an exponent of advanced ideological views, from an old comedy plot nothing short of a comprehensive coverage of the history of the 17th century.* Following a barrage of destructive and unfair criticism in 1952 the opera was forced off the repertoire. It was a long period of oblivion, a full fifteen years. It seemed that *Frol Skobeyev* would never stage a comeback. It was hardly ever mentioned by musicologists, some of whom pinned a label of "unstageable opera" on its score. And yet there were people who did not agree, and as it often happened with Khrennikov's music, they were men of the theatre. It was none other than director P. Zlatogorov who persuaded the opera's librettist and composer to take a fresh look at their creation.

After taking a long hard look at the original version of the opera, the authors edited out all that was nonessential to the opera's musical and dramatic basis, relieved it of excessive detail, didactic rhetoric, and made a few rearrangements. As a result, the musical fabric of the opera became lighter. The opera's principal character, Frol Skobeyev, was now more convincing. Finally, the new finale gave the opera better integrity and completeness. It now had a chorus at the end in praise of the joy of living and loving. It turned out that the librettist and the composer did not have to make major revisions after all but what they did do enabled the directors, actors and later the audiences to respond to it in a new way. Khrennikov changed the title from *Frol Skobeyev* to *The Low-born Son-in-Law,* which pointed up the democratic essence of the plot.

The Low-born Son-in-Law was accepted for production at two major theatres at once, one in Moscow and one in Novosibirsk. Interestingly, E. Fasenkov, who produced it in Novosibirsk, said at the time: *Our theatre has chosen this opera with good reason. Our repertoire policy is to give priority to everything topical, to raise the most burning issues of the day. And in* The Low-born Son-in-Law *with its atmospheric portrayal of the Russian way of life and immemorial Russian traditions we saw a work that would help us instill in the younger generations a sense of national pride, national identity and a caring attitude to the Russian cultural heritage. . .*

Ironically, a few years back these words about a comic opera based on a 17th-century plot would have sounded to some critics as paradoxical heresy. Now they were perfectly justified and Khrennikov's music gave ample grounds for that. The critics gave a most favorable assessment to the opera's first production in Novosibirsk. A. Dashicheva wrote in *Sovetskaya Kultura: What is it about this opera that makes it so fresh and*

The Low-born Son-in-Law, after initial difficulties, made a triumphant comeback in Novosibirsk and then in Moscow. The artistic potential of the opera was rich enough to allow for a variety of director's interpretations and treatments.

modern? It is, first of all, its music with its vivid imagery, original intonations, sincerity and warmth, the indestructible optimism of world outlook which is so close to us. At last the opinion of the critics coincided with the opinion of the audiences. A noted Siberian scholar, Professor Migerenko, summed up the latter thus: *The opera does not merely recreate a period of Russian history in a very atmospheric fashion but it is a truly national opera in the highest sense of the term. The composer is an acknowledged master of Russian folk melodies and has once again introduced many fresh folk elements into the opera.*

The opera's comeback was a triumph. Almost simultaneously with the Novosibirsk production *The Low-born Son-in-Law* was produced by Moscow's Nemirovich-Danchenko Musical Theatre. Other productions followed both in the USSR and in other countries. It was remarkable that the artistic potential of the original opera should have allowed for such a variety of director's approaches and treatments. The Moscow production emphasizes subtle psychological detail and attributes of domestic life, the color of the period (director P. Zlatogorov, conductor K. Abdullayev), in Novosibirsk the opera was produced as a merry play in the style of the wandering minstrels-cum-clowns-of-old which involved audience participation (director E. Fasenkov, conductor M. Buchbinder), the Kharkov production touched with a suggestion of traditional Russian vaudeville, emphasized the lyrical and poetical dimension of the opera (director L. Kukolev, conductor E. Dushenko). The new stage version produced by the Moscow Musical Theatre in 1979 (director M. Mordvinov, conductor V. Kozhuhar) also contained much that was new and fresh.

Songs and Films. . .

Generally speaking, I'm fond of writing film music, especially if the film has an important role for music. Writing film music appeals to me by virtue of the concrete purpose of my assignment, its specific imagery, characters and situations. I have been lucky to work with film directors who understand the role of music in films.

To get a better idea of the importance of films in Khrennikov's work, we should go back to the origins of his interest in film music, back to the 1930's. Nowadays writing music for a film is a routine, largely technical, task for most composers. The film director gives a composer "with a well practiced hand" a precise and limited assignment who then supplies the needed linking episodes of incidental music throwing in a couple of songs for good measure, sometimes nice, sometimes not so nice.

But in the age of the talkies, things were quite different. In those days composers explored with great enthusiasm the possibilities of the new medium of film music. Full-scale symphonic scores and song cycles were sometimes written for films and even quartets. Composers and motion-picture directors were searching for internal connections between picture and sound. Some of the world's best musicians wrote film music including Vaughan Williams and Gershwin, Jacques Ibert and Georges Auric, Benjamin Britten and Darius Milhaud, Hanns Eisler, Aaron Copland, and Arthur Honegger. They all enriched the language of the cinema while discovering new expressive possibilities in it for themselves.

Soviet composers were very much in the fore in this process of exploration and discovery. Even the venerable Ippolitov-Ivanov in his declining years wrote film music. The best pages of Soviet film music have been written by Shostakovich, Prokofiev, Khachaturyan and Dunayevsky. Prokofiev was Eisenstein's closest collaborator during work on the epic films *Alexander Nevsky* and *Ivan the Terrible.* Some of Shostakovich's film scores were perhaps as important for the composer as his major works. Dunayevsky was the founding father of a new genre—Soviet musical comedy film.

The hands of Tikhon Khrennikov playing. In the tradition of Rachmaninoff, Scriabin, Prokofiev and Shostakovich, Khrennikov is a superlative pianist and perhaps the best performer of his own compositions.

The name of Tikhon Khrennikov ranks next to those masters, both in terms of quantity and quality of his film music.

Films first attracted his attention in the mid-1930's. In one of his first press articles (April 1937) Khrennikov called the attention of the Composer's Union to film music. In 1938 he tried his hand for the first time in his score for the feature film *The Fight Goes On* based on Friedrich Wolf's anti-Fascist play *The Trojan Horse*. But his first really significant work for the cinema was his score for the film *The Swineherd and the Shepherd*.

In August 1939, G. Khubov wrote in the newspaper *Kino (Film): It is to be hoped that new musical films of both the epic and lyrical variety will appear in the near future along with musical comedies, operettas and vaudevilles. We should make this idea interesting to our leading film directors such as Dovzhenko, Pudovkin, Eisenstein whose films are remarkable for their intrinsic musical quality and the symphonic character of their composition. We should persuade our composers Khachaturyan, Shostakovich, Khrennikov, Dzerzhinski, Dunayevsky, Prokofiev, Shaporin to write more film music. It is important to ensure that profound penetration and musical treatment be organically integrated with the films' dramatic development. This is a challenging but also an exciting task!*

Among those who were the first to meet the challenge were film director Ivan Pyriev and composer Tikhon Khrennikov.

Early in January 1941, Pyriev said: *We are soon beginning to shoot the first episodes of* The Swineherd and the Shepherd *written by V. Gusev, soon. Music, songs and country ditties in this film will be more than illustrative musical inserts. Like in opera, singing and music constitute its basic fabric, so in our film choral singing, duets and arias form an organic component of its plot. Tikhon Khrennikov is writing the musical score for the film.*"

The ideological and artistic concept of the film was fresh and original. The film makers were completely independent as they ventured out on an untrodden path paying no attention to the traditional devices of operetta. Nor did they copy the popular foreign film musicals starring Francesca Gall and Deanna Durbin, which centered around two or three hit songs.

The film's rich musicality was preconceived by its director and script writer and the character of its musicality was fully consonant with Khrennikov's original talent. *The Swineherd and the Shepherd* was profoundly national in character. The sources of its music were Russian songs and Russian folklore.

The film was released in the early days of the war and was a great success. Using interesting dramatic material and drawing on the intonational wealth of urban and rural folklore, Khrennikov gave the film's heroes unique musical characterizations. The film had tremendous human appeal. The melodies were noted for a charming tunefulness born of the poetry of country life. Khrennikov's musical style and his gentle charm were unmistakable throughout. The composer chose a popular waltz form for the *Song about Moscow*, the film's leitmotif. This lent the patriotic song a special soft charm and a sincere melodic quality.

Since then the film made by Pyriev, Gusev and Khrennikov has been shown all over the Soviet Union and in many cities of Europe and America. Lev Kassil was right in predicting a long life for its music.

Many famous twentieth-century composers, including Mikhail Ippolitov-Ivanov (top), Georges Auric (bottom), Aaron Copland (top, facing page) and Benjamin Britten (bottom, facing page), wrote music for films, as did Tikhon Khrennikov.

Even today this film is regarded by many as a marvelously integrated musical-dramatic masterpiece, just as it was seen by Soviet audiences in the early 1940s. Two decades after the film's release, noted film critic R. Yurenyev defined it as "a comic film opera". We feel that a more precise definition would be a "film musical", the first of its kind in Soviet motion picture history.

The next film made by the same team *At 6 p.m. After the War*, followed the pattern set by *The Swineherd and The Shepherd*. Although it dealt with a wartime theme, the new film was projected into the postwar peaceful future. And again its romantic poetic mood sprang from Tikhon Khrennikov's musical score.

For once the critics were unanimous in their favorable assessment of the film, which was rare. B. Borisov writing in *Krasnaya Zvezda*, the army newspaper, observed that Khrennikov's music *does not merely illustrate the film but is, in fact, an integral part of it. The songs and the recitative in it constitute a single musical-poetical stream all through the film.* Grigory Alexandrov, a noted film director, was of the same opinion: *The film's music forms an organic component of its dramatic design and is an interesting artistic phenomenon in its own right.*

. . .On Victory Day, May 8, 1979 the film *At 6 p.m. After the War* was shown on Soviet television for the umpteenth time. Despite the lapse of decades, TV-viewers across the USSR thoroughly enjoyed it, appreciating particularly its ever green tunes which were a subtle tool for revealing the intrinsic dramatic pattern of the film and the inner world of its main characters.

Indeed, as we watch this film today we are amazed at its makers' bold approach to describing events of the war in a film musical at the height of that war with total truthfulness and in a suitably elevated style. It was a pioneering approach as the war theme did not really reach Soviet musical theatres until two decades later. . . Victor Gusev wrote: *There is a real poet in Pyriev. He approaches his hero as a poet, seeing life through the eyes and responsive heart of a real artist.* The same fully applies to Tikhon Khrennikov. It was significant that the creative cooperation of these two artists should have proved so productive. Shostakovich once said: *The successful cooperation of film director Ivan Pyriev and composer Tikhon Khrennikov has given us not only excellent films which our people love but also songs which they sing.*

Khrennikov maintained his film connection through the late 1940s and the early 1950s when he cooperated with two other film directors: he wrote music for Yuli Reizman's films *The Train Goes East* and *The Holder of the Gold Star*; for L. Lukov, he wrote the score for the film *The Coalminers of Donetsk*. These films were full of music, good music, too. The acting, directing and camera work were also good, but the screenplays left much to be desired and so the films did not have a successful run. Only some of their songs remained popular for a while after the films were gone from the screen. Incidentally, Khrennikov made his debut as an actor in one of those films.

Director Yuli Reizman had been looking for the right actor for the role of a sailor who was supposed to sing one of the songs. The filming period was drawing to a close but no suitable actor materialized. Reizman gave up the search and asked Khrennikov to do his song himself. After a cou-

ple of takes, the composer recorded the song to his own accompaniment on the accordion. Reizman liked it and proceeded to film the whole episode. Everything went smoothly. The director was pleased and later so were the audiences.

This was his first and last appearance in films. Khrennikov himself joked about it: *I'm afraid I was not cut out to be a film star.* Perhaps not, but this episode did show the composer's pretty wide range of ability, often in unexpected directions. And everywhere his sincere and open-hearted personality comes across, as it certainly did in that episode.

Since the end of the last war, television with a steadily expanding audience has been rapidly gaining ascendancy among the mass media. Television has provided an excellent vehicle for communication between people in the arts and the public at large. Khrennikov, with his keen sense of the present has always been sensitive and responsive to the demands of the day and the needs of the people. He became a regular contributor to television films and serials by way of compensation for his failure to find sufficiently rewarding material in the cinema. In his work for television he displayed his usual well-developed sense of responsibility, a high professional standard, an innovative approach and a firm refusal to fall in with the vagaries of current fashion. Among the more successful TV-films for which Khrennikov wrote scores two stand out—the musical comedy *La Cagnotte* after Eugine Labiche and *The Duenna* after Richard Sheridan. The music of these two is fully within the tradition of Khrennikov's scores for films and plays of the 1930's, noted for its relaxed gaiety, a vivid melodic pattern, graphic images and characterizations and, most importantly, organic unity of action, lyrics and music.

Tikhon Khrennikov made his first —and only—appearance on the screen as a musically inclined sailor in Yuli Reizman's film *A Train Goes East*, for which he composed the score.

A Life for the People

Undoubtedly, involvement in public affairs, meeting people in different walks of life on a regular basis, although it does take up quite a lot of one's time, enlarges one's horizons. Musicians are no exception. I have no regrets that my life and career have taken the course they did. It seems to me that our time, our Soviet reality demand that a person engaged in the arts combine his creative pursuits with public affairs activity. For me personally this is not even a duty but a natural vital need. This need has been instilled in us by the climate of our national life, by the entire history of the Soviet state and specifically of the Soviet artistic scene.

In 1948, the First All-Union Congress of Composers elected Tikhon Khrennikov Secretary-General of the Union of Soviet Composers. For many and not just for outside observers, this came as rather a surprise. He was only thirty-five at the time. Now the period of the late 40s, as we all know, was a particularly difficult time in the history of Soviet art, a time of reappraisal of values and personalities, a reappraisal, let us face it, not always objective or fair.

And yet Khrennikov's election seemed unexpected only at first sight. His prestige within the musical community was sufficiently high, backed up by not a few talented compositions. Then again, the composer's public-spirited temperament had by then become clearly pronounced. This kind of temperament was the mark of a man of firm beliefs, a man with the courage of his convictions, who adhered to high principles, opposed extremes and knew how to tackle the most complex and, at times, quite awkward and delicate problems.

Khrennikov did acquire these qualities early in his youth. He first displayed them in 1936 when after graduating from the Moscow Conservatory, he entered the highly intense artistic atmosphere of the pre-war period. For the first time his voice was heard publicly during the discussion that followed the publication in *Pravda* of the notorious article entitled *Cacophony Instead of Music* and *A False Ballet,* which harshly and unfairly criticized the work of Shostakovich. The discussion was characterized by excessive and misplaced zeal, acrimony, rushing to extremes and revival of nihilistic views. Both justified and unjustified accusations were levelled against several composers. Against this polemic background, the attitude of Khrennikov, fresh out of the Conservatory, was noted for a calm and constructive tone. Personal attacks and baiting were distasteful to the young composer who showed concern for the morrow of Soviet music. Characteristically, Khrennikov strongly opposed those who, under the pretext of advocating realism in music, sought to relegate to the background, if not dismiss altogether as unimportant, matters of professional skill and the technical arsenal of composers. Questions of musical technology were even then seen by Khrennikov as being closely bound up with the ideological content of music. He emphasized: *Isolated and pitiful, indeed, were the voices of those few contributors to this discussion who claimed quite groundlessly, that the writing of fugues and 16-voice counterpoints by students of the Conservatory allegedly leads to formalism. I think we should nip this mindless twaddle in the bud for it confuses young musicians as regards the need to study hard and master essential technical procedures and approaches without which no one can hope to become a real composer. You will recall that Rimsky-Korsakov, Tchaikovsky and other great composers of the past did not find that the study of counterpoint and the writing of fugues got in the way of creating good music. On the contrary, it helped them gain more confidence, technical brilliance and discipline. Who will say that our young musicians and composers can do without these qualities? But beyond that, we have to work hard at raising our cultural standard, to enlarge our ideological and political horizons, all of which is essential for genuinely creative Soviet artists. Unfortunately, the Conservatory has so far given us little help in this respect. Therefore, the entire pattern of the educational process at the Conservatory should be redesigned to ensure that it graduates musicians are well-equipped for attempting to create*

At the Second Congress of the USSR Composers' Union in the Column Hall of the House of the Unions. Front row, left to right: Vano Muradeli, Georgi Sviridov, Dmitri Shostakovich, Aram Khachaturian, Tikhon Khrennikov, Dmitri Kabalevsky. Standing in the back, left to right: President Leonid I. Brezhnev, Prime Minister Alexei Kosygin, Minister of Culture Pyotr Demichev.

those "towering masterpieces" of Soviet art of which Neuhaus spoke so well. Our young composers in this effect should aim at rich emotionality, passion, greater melodic expressiveness and tunefulness. The watchword inscribed on our banner should be—Down with formalism, imitation and epigonism! Up with original, vivid, full-blooded, and expressive music!

From then on Khrennikov made public statements on topical issues of musical life and creativity more or less on a regular basis. Later in 1936 the *Sovetskoye Isskustvo* newspaper carried his article on the work of the Composers' Union. Khrennikov urged for closer attention to the creative activities of the Union's membership, above all, of the young composers who had to be encouraged in every way, notably by commissioning them to write music on various themes in different genres, and by regular discussion of finished compositions. He also called for further development of Soviet opera and symphonic music.

After he had graduated from the Moscow Conservatory, Khrennikov began to publish articles and reviews on a regular basis. In particular, he wrote reviews on a series of opera productions and concertos and commented on major events on the musical scene. Besides, he was actively involved in the many-sided activities of the Composers' Union. Not a single burning issue of the day escaped his attention or left him indifferent. And by no means did he always join the chorus of those who voiced "the general opinion" even if some of the more authoritative of his fellow composers did. When in April 1937 it was proposed to set up a Union of Soviet Musicians, (instead of the Composers' Union), Khrennikov was among the few opponents of the idea. He produced cogent arguments. *I do not think it advisable to create a unified Union of Musicians. I am afraid it will be a quite unnecessary branch of the already existing Union. Composers have their own set of specific interests and so do the performers. What is the point of creating a new organization which will bring all musicians together? The authors of the article 'A Union of Soviet Musicians is a Must' are advocating universalism for the sake of universalism."*

Khrennikov cited the works of Nikolai Myaskovsky (top) and Vano Muradeli (bottom) as examples of "the exceptional wealth and rich diversity of individual styles and treatment characterizing Soviet musical creativity."

Developing his ideas on the structure and the tasks of the Composers' Union, which was still in its formative stage, Khrennikov continued: *It would be good for the musicologists and music critics to join the Composers' Union. The point is not yet another restructuring but whether we can breathe life into the already existing association of composers and music critics. For the performers we should create a new union. All these matters bear, of course, on the activities of our concert organizations. But the creation of a unified union of musicians will not eliminate, once and for all, the shortcomings and drawbacks in this area.*

Many of the ideas that Khrennikov first voiced in 1937 have not lost their relevance to this day. As for the proposed unified musicians' union, Khrennikov's arguments must have been quite convincing, for the idea was abandoned.

In 1939-1940 Khrennikov found himself at the center of yet another heated debate on the future of Soviet music. The debate was triggered by the publication in the government daily *Izvestia* of an article by Khrennikov and I. Dzerzhinski summing up the results of the completed ten-day festival of Soviet music. The gist of that article was the authors' strong defense of the right of each artist to follow his own way. *Listen to the best works of Prokofiev, Koval, Myaskovski, Khachaturyan, Shostakovich and Muradeli and you will appreciate the exceptional wealth and rich*

*diversity of individual styles and treatment characterizing Soviet musical
creativity today. This is all to the good. The worst enemy of art is standard-
ized, stereotyped approach, mediocrity and sterile complacency. We Soviet
artists have a common goal in creating the art of socialist realism of a high
standard. But different artists work towards this goal in different ways. We
are convinced that truly talented artists should follow their unique paths
towards the common objective.*

Khrennikov's press articles and contributions to public debates made a
substantial impact on the musical scene of the day.

The foregoing shows that Tikhon Khrennikov exhibited quite a
vigorous temperament in public affairs and musical life in the pre-war
years. And it is hardly surprising that he should have been elected
Secretary-General of the Union of Soviet Composers after the war. The
still young musician faced a difficult and responsible task—all the more
so since he took over from Academician Asafiev, the experienced and
respected doyen of the Soviet musical community who had been gravely
ill and died in 1949.

Gian-Carlo Menotti, one of the many foreign musicians of distinction who were close personal friends of Tikhon Khrennikov.

As Secretary-General of the Union of Soviet Composers, Tikhon Khrennikov has many duties to attend to. Here he is shown inspecting, with Dmitri Shostakovich, the new premises of the Composers' Union in Moscow, in 1963.

The congress of Soviet composers which elected Tikhon Khrennikov Secretary-General of the Composers' Union met in the spring of 1948 soon after the publication of the Resolution of the Central Committee of the CPSU "On V. Muradeli's Opera *A Great Friendship*." This document, which restated the fundamental ideological and aesthetic principles of Soviet art—realism, popular spirit, democratic nature—also contained erroneous assessments and denounced some of the leading Soviet musicians for formalism. These unfair accusations sprang from the climate of subjectivist opinion generated by Stalin's personality cult. Ten years later, of course, the Central Committee of the CPSU disavowed those mistaken assessments but the damage had been done. In the late 1940's, the atmosphere within the composers' community was rather tense, not to say nervous. Inevitably in this atmosphere egos were hurt, attempts made by some unscrupulous persons to take advantage of the situation to pay off old scores and, as a result, personal animosities arose and quite unnecessary conflicts developed.

The new Secretary-General of the Composers' Union had to show tact, consideration, and strict adherence to high principles. He had to display a caring attitude to talent, broad-mindedness and leadership to be a good diplomat, in order to induce the composers to join forces and work together towards their common, truly creative objectives. Indeed Khrennikov had a difficult task before him as attempts were being made by some crusading bureaucrats to isolate and even excommunicate from the mainstream of musical life the so-called "formalists" and to strike their compositions off the concert hall repertoire. The young secretary-general of the Composers' Union deserved a lot of credit for preventing just that.

Pitchforked into the middle of a difficult situation, he took his bearings with surprising confidence and speed. His public statements and press articles struck a distinctly businesslike and constructive note. He would give his backing without hesitation to everything that was new and talented. He promoted the works of the best composers, including those who had been censured in the abovementioned Central Committee resolution. He also encouraged and promoted the creative explorations of the younger generation of Soviet composers and musicians. He worked hard to consolidate the Composers' Union. Everything he did in those difficult days for the Soviet musical community stamped him as a wise strategist and a far-seeing leader, who put the honor and future of Soviet music before "esprit de corps".

Tikhon Khrennikov has achieved something that is unprecedented in the history of Soviet music, if only on the administrative side. He has been the permanent Secretary-General of the Union of Soviet Composers for thirty-five years now, the longest-running tenure of office of anyone. At the five successive composers' congresses held since 1948, his colleagues have reelected him as their leader, a tribute to his fine human qualities, organizational talent and, last but not least, his prestige as a musician. And each time he has fully lived up to their expectations. In 1963, Yuri Shaporin, a prominent composer, wrote: *For fifteen years now Khrennikov has been the worthy leader of the multi-national Soviet musical community, providing an example of genuine democracy in action, kindness, generosity and comradely attention to and consideration for every member of the Union, for our numerous foreign friends.* Ten years later Yevgeny Svetlanov, of another generation, echoed Shaporin when he said: *There is hardly anyone in our Union who does not hold Tikhon Nikolayevich in high regard. And we all know that managing a giant association of creative people, such as ours, is not easy. He has a genius for bringing together people with different tastes and artistic attachments and dissimilar musical styles. It is difficult to pool their efforts without hurting anyone's pride, without imposing your own ideas of music and your own perceptions. To direct the creative energy of each member of the Union towards a common goal—to create music with a lofty Communist message, is a mission that few can cope with. And the fact that Tikhon Nikolayevich has performed as well as he has done for as long as he has, earned him great prestige and respect.*

Foremost Soviet conductor **Yevgeny Svetlanov who conducted performances of many works by Khrennikov.**

An outsider cannot imagine the amount of time, energy and worry that the demanding job of the head of the Composers' Union takes daily, and even hourly. For Khrennikov this is not in any sense a function confined to putting in an obligatory appearance at ceremonies, anniversary banquets and other similar glittering occasions, or signing important documents. As he sees it, he has to give his attention to everything, to be everywhere his presence is required, to delve into all sorts of questions, both routine and of global importance, relating to the common good and affecting only individuals. Khrennikov is a good listener who quickly latches on to the essence of what he hears on all sides in order to draw proper conclusions. He is one of the rare breed of men who combine successfully creative pursuits and the intensive activities of a public man.

Everyday Tikhon Khrennikov, a composer of world renown, comes to his office in Nezhdanova Street as any government employee. The only difference perhaps is that he does not turn up early in the morning,

devoting the "morning stint" to writing music. Every day of the week except Tuesdays (the day he teaches at the Moscow Conservatory) his smallish office is usually crowded. If he makes an appointment, he keeps it even though some unexpected and urgent matter may delay his arrival. If he makes a promise, he keeps it. Tikhon Khrennikov tries to give his attention to everyone who needs it and to help everyone, if he can. That is just the sort of man he is. . .

On Mondays, the Composers' Union Secretariat meets in regular session, usually with Khrennikov in the chair. They have to deal with a host of questions ranging from arranging music festivals to planning the next month's schedule of auditions of new compositions. Often matters relating to musical creativity, music education and art appreciation are included in the agenda at Khrennikov's initiative. Sitting in the Secretariat sessions are often representatives of concert organizations, government ministries, radio and television, publishing houses, newspapers and magazines. The atmosphere is always businesslike, informal and relaxed. Khrennikov will never demean himself by a perfunctory reply, either verbal or written, to any inquiry. A veteran of the Secretariat in more than one sense, he is still one of its more energetic members when it comes to raising new issues or contributing to the ensuing discussion. He is also an easy man to make a quick start in response to an invitation to travel somewhere across half the country to attend a conference of local composers or to take part in some event arranged by the local branch of the Composers' Union.

Once every five years, when the Soviet Union's Communists meet in the Moscow Kremlin for a regular Party congress, they pay tribute to his valuable services to the country by electing him to important party bodies. Since 1961, Khrennikov has been elected to the Central Auditing Commission of the CPSU three times. At the 25th and 26th Congresses, in 1976 and 1981 he was elected an alternate (non-voting) member of the CPSU Central Committee. On both occasions he addressed Congress delegates from the platform. After each Party Congress, Khrennikov meets his colleagues from the Composers' Union Secretariat and board and later all the members of the Moscow branch of the Union, to share with them his impressions of the Congress and to discuss ways of implementing the Congress's decisions within their organization. Another facet of Khrennikov the public man is his work as deputy to the Supreme Soviet of the USSR, the Soviet Parliament. He was first elected to the Supreme Soviet of the Russian Federation over thirty years ago. In 1961 he was elected deputy to the Supreme Soviet of the USSR. Since then he has widely travelled to meet his constituents in the Novgorod and Smolensk regions and, more recently, in Dagestan. He receives many different people who come to him for help, advice, or support. He also gets thousands of letters annually from his electors who write about their concerns or problems.

. . .Indeed it would be difficult to say where Khrennikov the musician ends and Khrennikov the public man begins. It is just as difficult to say when his day's work ends and his private life begins. Even those people who at different times had an opportunity to approach him for advice or help, and who have invariably received his close attention and assistance would find it difficult to answer that question. You can phone Khrennikov at home any time of the day or night and you will hear at the other end of the line the friendly voice of either the man himself or his wife, Clara Arnoldovna, who takes as much credit as the host for the invariably friendly and informal atmosphere reigning in their home.

Tikhon Khrennikov addressing the Conference for World Peace. Khrennikov's dedication to the cause of better relations between all the countries of the world has also been expressed in his very successful efforts to expand the international contacts of Soviet musicians.

Tikhon and Klara Khrennikov, a happy couple whose golden anniversary is not so far away.

French composer Andre Jolivet, a good friend of Tikhon Khrennikov's.

They have been happily married for almost half a century now. It is probably not easy to be the wife of a man as busy and generous as her husband. It is difficult to give even an approximate estimate of how many people are grateful to Clara Arnoldovna for her help and support, her advice and attention. Visitors to their home include prominent musicians, poets, painters, public leaders as well as people from ordinary walks of life. Also foreign guests and many young people. Everybody finds a friendly, relaxed atmosphere and feels very much at home. The hosts are always their natural selves, hospitable and gracious people with no pretense or plastic smiles. In their home distinctions of status, position in society or age quickly vanish.

Our thumbnail sketch of Tikhon Khrennikov, the man, will not be complete if we fail to mention the tremendous contribution he has made to enhancing the status of Soviet music worldwide, to the maintenance and expansion of the international contacts of Soviet musicians. One form of these contacts is the holding of festivals of Soviet music in different countries and reciprocal festivals of foreign music in the USSR. Another is all 'round cooperation between Soviet musicians and their counterparts in other socialist countries, the holding of major international music competitions and conferences. Finally, there are regular concert tours of the Soviet Union by some of the world's foremost musicians. Georges Auric, Zoltán Kodály, Benjamin Britten, Samuel Barber, Roy Harris, André Jolivet, Gian-Carlo Menotti, Pancho Vladigerov, Lubomir Pipkov, Eugen Suchon, Václav Dobias and Paul Dessau are only some of the many eminent musicians from around the world who have been Khrennikov's guests to become his close personal friends and

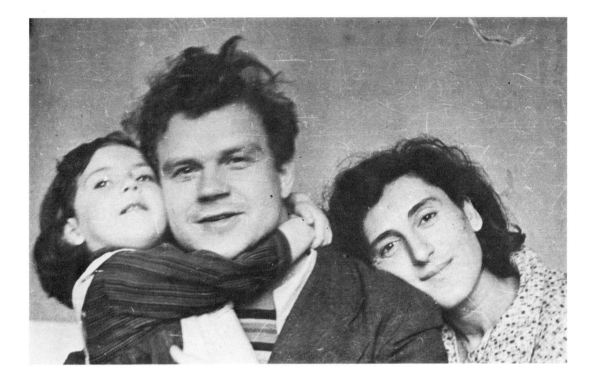

Portrait of the composer as a
family man. Top: with wife Clara
and daughter Natasha. Bottom:
many years later, the Khrennikovs with grandson Andrei.

With conductor Pietro Argento, one of Tikhon Khrennikov's Italian admirers who has done much to promote his works. Khrennikov is Chairman of the Soviet-Italian Parliamentary Group and is probably one of the most popular foreign musicians in Italy.

Remarkable Brazilian composer Heitor Villa-Lobos.

friends of Soviet music. Perhaps contacts between Soviet musicians and their Italian counterparts should be singled out for special mention. Since the Supreme Soviet of the USSR appointed Tikhon Khrennikov Chairman of the Soviet-Italian Parliamentary Group, he has made frequent visits to Italy, either as a concert pianist or as part of various Soviet delegations, and, more recently, also as a member of the jury of international music competitions in Rome and Terni and as a delegate to various symposia and conferences. It would be no exaggeration to say that few foreign musicians are as well-loved or well-known in Italy as Tikhon Khrennikov. One evidence of this is the election of Khrennikov some years ago as an honorary member of Italy's prestigious Academia Tiberiana. Khrennikov has done much to introduce the music of contemporary Italian composers to Soviet audiences. Needless to say, he has many friends in Italy, as indeed in other countries, among the foremost musicians who include Virgilio Mortari, Mario Zafred, Franco Maninno and the late and lamented Nino Rota. . . Franco Maninno wrote ten years ago: *The high quality of his music has long been appreciated by cultural leaders in many countries. Khrennikov is a worthy successor to the great classics of Russian music. His music, it seems to me, is born in the depths of his soul. We value highly both his inspiration and his professional skill. Listeners are enchanted by the natural beauty of Khrennikov's compositions with their remarkable combination of talent and musical erudition. . . I may consider myself lucky as I know Khrennikov, the composer, and Khrennikov, the man. He is my dear friend. Whenever I see him I admire his big-hearted generosity, his sincerity and humanity. He is a model for all of us musicians.* Not long ago we asked Franco Maninno: *"What has changed since then?"* He replied: *"Nothing, except that our friendship has become stronger. . ."*

Two of the outstanding Russian musicians who were fated to settle for good in foreign countries were grateful to Khrennikov for his attention and help. It was none other than Khrennikov who, in 1961 while on a

Tikhon Khrennikov greets one of the great masters of Russian music, Igor Stravinsky, at Stravinsky's recital in the Great Hall of the Conservatory, in 1962.

Pietro Argento awarding the diploma of Honorary Member of Italy's prestigious Academia Tiberiana to Tikhon Khrennikov. This honor testifies to the popularity that Khrennikov's works enjoy in Italy. Below: Khrennikov's Academia Tiberiana diploma.

visit to the United States, called on the aging Igor Stravinsky. This meeting resulted in a historic reunion of the Russian musician of genius with his country of origin, after fifty years of separation. Another great man of Russian music, Alexander Tscherepnin, was able to visit his country thanks to Khrennikov's efforts. In 1965 he wrote a letter to him expressing a fervent desire to visit the USSR. As Tcherepnin recalled it later: *My long-cherished dream came true thanks to Khrennikov's responsiveness and his big-hearted hospitality.* These are just two examples out of many. . .

What is it that motivates Tikhon Khrennikov in his unflagging activities to strengthen and expand contacts between Soviet composers and their counterparts in the rest of the world? The best answer to this question has been given by the man himself: *My aim and objective is to emphasize that in this day and age the maintenance and expansion of contacts between Soviet musicians and the progressive-minded men of the arts around the world takes on a special importance. It helps strengthen the position of genuine realist art, and advance the struggle against the musical dross with which the 'avant-garde' musicians of every hue and shade have been polluting the world's concert halls and stages. So it is not just a matter of demonstrating the creative achievements but it also involves a polemic over matters of principle in which we are called upon to represent Soviet art with maximum conviction, to uphold our humanistic ideals and esthetic values and positions. . . We know many wonderful artists in other countries who adhere to sound principles in the development of contemporary art and who, in their innovative quests, rely on the great traditions of the past and are responsive to the burning issues of the day. It is their work that we try to present as fully as possible to Soviet audiences and they gladly come to the USSR*

121

Top: A meeting with Artur Rubinstein. Bottom: Peter Mennin and Tikhon Khrennikov at the opening of the First International Music Festival in 1981. Khrennikov was, in a way, the spirit behind the event.

"We know many wonderful artists in other countries. . .and they gladly come to the USSR in response to our invitations." Paul Robeson, here shown with Tikhon Khrennikov and his colleagues at the USSR Union of Composers, was one of them.

in response to our invitations. On the other hand, festivals of Soviet music and foreign tours by Soviet musicians, according to our foreign colleagues, help them in their own struggle for real art, for establishing true artistic values.

The international music festival held in the spring of 1981 was designed to promote these lofty goals. The idea of this festival was first put forward by Tikhon Khrennikov at the time of the 25th Congress of the CPSU. His initiative met with enthusiastic and widespread support. The festival which brought together some of the best musicians of our time was a full-scale review of twentieth century music and had wide repercussions throughout the world. Khrennikov, who was chairman of the festival's organizing committee, devoted the whole of his enthusiasm, energy and ardor of his soul to this wonderful project.

Rodion Shchedrin wrote at the time: *We should all consider ourselves lucky. I think that the helmsman of the USSR Composers' Union takes personal credit for the spectacular success of Soviet music over the past fifteen years. For many years I have been fortunate to observe him in action almost daily, and as I often work closely with him I am perhaps better placed than anyone to see this in 'close-up', as it were. What makes Tikhon Nikolayevich such a dynamic and efficient leader? It is, above all, a rare combination of the prestige and authority of a great musician, and of endearing human qualities. It is his rare talent to be happy to see the victories and successes scored by his colleagues, fellow musicians. He applauds them all sincerely. He also follows the work of others with close interest. He has a rare ability to perceive objectively what he hears, rather than through the "ear" of his stylistic preferences. He is a sincere well-wisher. His reactions are super-quick and he usually grasps the essence of what he hears instantly, from "a quarter tone", as it were. Tikhon Khrennikov is a wise strategist with a wealth of experience in human communication. He never panics, no matter how difficult the situation may be. he also has an incredible and happy ability to get his second wind just when he needs it. It seems to me sometimes that the sheer complexity of the many duties this man has to perform is too much for anyone to cope with single-handed, unless he can live a whole week in one day. But then I remember the punchline of an old saying: ". . .He that sows character shall reap a life worth living."*

Music for the People

There was a period in my career when I concentrated on the vocal genres, opera and musical comedy, and wrote a lot of music for films and stage plays. Now I am more attracted to instrumental and symphonic music. . . I am now writing more music for orchestra and orchestra with solo instruments. I think my Second Concerto *and my* Third Symphony *reflect fairly accurately my musical philosophy today. The main thing for me now is not questions of composing style or virtuosity of performance (although these are not unimportant in this context) but rather the range of my emotional moods in recent years.*

You may well ask why after such a long break Tikhon Khrennikov has again turned to an area of musical creativity which he seemed to have long neglected. The reasons are many, including the need to renew his creative arsenal, and even external, non-musical factors. . . Apparently at some point he felt the need to express himself in instrumental music and those musicologists who had without hesitation pigeonholed him as a vocal music composer must have provided the right kind of "irritant" to push him in this direction. Then his contacts with outstanding performing artists who had always shown a lively interest in his work also influenced the direction of his creative quests. But there was one other factor—his own activity as a performer, his own highly artistic nature.

Khrennikov had always found playing the piano before an audience a thoroughly enjoyable experience. But the way things shaped up, especially in the immediate post-war years and later, he found it difficult, if not impossible, to give piano recitals regularly. And on those rare occasions when he did appear in concerts, he accompanied singers who performed his romances, arias from his operas or his songs. He was brilliant on such occasions. His cooperation with vocalists always brought them joy and stimulation them. Georgi Dudarev, one of Khrennikov's long-time partners wrote some twenty years ago: *Khrennikov is a very sensitive and subtle accompanist of his own compositions. Personally, I enjoy appearing with him. He infects you with his own temperament so much that you can shake off your tiredness and even indisposition which often afflicts singers. It is a have a lot to learn from his artistry and his modest, perfectly natural and relaxed stage manner.* Later Dudarev was echoed by Yevgeny Svetlanov,

Receiving guests from abroad: Tikhon Khrennikov with Artur Rubinstein (top) and Igor Stravinsky (bottom). Stravinsky's historic visit to his native land was largely the result of his meeting with Khrennikov in the United States in 1961.

the conductor: *Khrennikov's accompaniment is a close creative alliance between composer and performer, an ensemble that happens right before the eyes of the audience as a result of the intimate understanding of the performer's individuality by the composer-accompanist. Khrennikov feels well the performing artist's creative potential, having discussed and rehearsed everything with him before the concert. On stage Tikhon Nikolayevich is careful not to cramp the performer's style. Even in the simplest piano accompaniment he can display his creative fantasy to the full.*

The steadily growing popularity of Khrennikov, the composer, brought Khrennikov, the pianist, back to the concert platform. Since the late 1950's Khrennikov's piano recitals have been more regular both at major concert halls in the Soviet Union and later abroad. Whereas in the past he would usually give them at club houses, appearing before chamber audiences, these days he usually performs before philharmonic audiences. It is difficult to pinpoint exactly when the change occurred. Perhaps the turning point was that concert in Saratov at which his *Second Symphony,* the *Suite* from *Much Ado About Nothing,* Ordyn Nashokin's monologue from the comic opera *Frol Skobeyev,* Frol Baijev's aria from the opera *In Storm,* and romances and songs were performed. The Saratov Philharmonic was conducted on that occasion by the experienced Natan Faktorovich, and the soloist was the young but already well-known Bulgarian bass Nicolai Ghiaurov who has since been one of the admirers and best interpreters of Khrennikov's music. Shortly after the Saratov concert, Natan Faktorovich wrote Khrennikov: *Please accept our sincere and warm congratulations and our thanks. People in our city are talking about nothing else but you and Nicolai Ghiaurov. The pictures are ready and Ghiaurov has been given one copy of each. . . Saratov has never accorded such a warm welcome to anyone.*

But during the Saratov concert the composer confined himself to being a member of the audience and the program was rather limited. It was apparently this occasion that provided an additional incentive for Khrennikov to go into another round of public appearances, both as composer and performer. Indeed, he was writing new major instrumental compositions while appearing on the concert platform, more often than not, as an interpreter of his *First Piano Concerto.*

In early January 1961, a Moscow newspaper carried a brief item entitled *Tikhon Khrennikov does the Solo* which said: *Perhaps not all of our music lovers are aware that one of our foremost composers Tikhon Khrennikov, before the war studied two disciplines at the Moscow Conservatory: composition and piano technique. Soon Moscow audiences will again hear Khrennikov's First Piano concerto as performed by the composer in the Grand Hall of the Conservatory. Music lovers in Kishinyov, however, have been more lucky as they are already enjoying Tikhon Khrennikov's piano recitals in the Moldavian capital where he was invited to attend the première of his opera* In Storm *produced by the Moldavian Opera House. He will appear on January 11 as a pianist in a concert made up of his piano compositions in the hall of the local Philharmonic Society.* A few days later the leading newspaper in Moldavia wrote: *Tikhon Khrennikov is a master pianist with a convincing and powerful technique and a subtle interpretative skill. He sustains his inspiration throughout the four movements of his Concerto. Thanks to his vivid performance, the Concerto had a refreshingly effective sound.*

Khrennikov with Bulgarian bass Nikolai Ghiaurov.

The composer at the piano in his study—"a master pianist with a convincing and powerful technique and a subtle interpretative skill," according to a review.

Tikhon Khrennikov and his long-time friend and collaborator Leonid Kogan congratulating great pianist Emil Gilels on his success after one of his concerts.

Distinguished Soviet pianist and teacher Lev Oborin.

This opened a new chapter in Khrennikov's career. He was now an acknowledged performer. But the same period also saw a new chapter in his work as a composer which, predictably enough, was primarily associated with his work in the concerto and instrumental genre.

The idea of writing a violin concerto was suggested to him by Leonid Kogan, the violinist. Close cooperation of major composers and performers is a productive tradition of long standing in Soviet music. Examples include the frequent cooperation between Prokofiev and Myaskovsky, Shostakovich and Khachaturyan, on the one hand, and Mravinski, Oborin, Oistrakh and Gilels, on the other. The alliance of Khrennikov and Kogan is in keeping with this tradition. Kogan recalled: *I once dropped a hint to Tikhon Nikolayevich that perhaps it would be a good idea for him to write a violin concerto. He replied: 'Actually I've been thinking about it myself and perhaps I will get around to it before long.' This was in the winter of 1959. By the summer of that year the Concerto was all but ready. I recall how I came to see him then and how he showed me his new composition with his characteristic enthusiasm and exhilaration, playing and singing the violin part. I immediately took a liking to the Concerto with its ingenuous freshness and technical complexity which, even in the author's treatment were apparent. The surprising thing was that, although Tikhon Nikolayevich had never played the violin, it was very much a violin-tailored concerto. It is quite an achievement since I know from experience that you may know the violin well and may even play it well and yet fail to write for the instrument well. Of course, during our joint work on the Concerto we did some focussing in the texture of the solo part, but even so, as I said, the original version of the Concerto was remarkably organic. In the autumn of 1959 I played it in Moscow and later in many of the world's major concert halls. I've also made a recording of the Concerto.*

Khrennikov's debut in the new genre was an unqualified success. Proof of that was the interest the *Concerto* excited among violinists. Before long the list of the first performers of the *Concerto* was joined by Igor Bezrodny, Victor Pikalsen, Eduard Gratch, Vladimir Spivakov, Ioko Sato and the youthful Pavel Kogan. The composition received a good press. Its appearance and the fact that Khrennikov turned to the concerto genre after such a long break was greeted both by critics and by fellow composers. Mikhail Tshulaki, former director of the Bolshoi Theatre, wrote: *The new* violin Concerto *is notable for its rich melody and a sense of the living breath of life.* The reviewers pointed out the lightness and ease of the Concerto's harmonic language, its exquisite texture, diversity of orchestral colors and the overall cheerful tone. I. Martinov commented: *"This cheerful mood dominates the opening bars where against the background of clearly rhythmic chords of the orchestra the resolute and purposeful sound of the main theme is heard. A sense of emotional elevation is still with us as we follow the composer from one episode to the next. We hear the tuneful secondary theme with its unexpected intonational shifts and later, the flowing, serene music of the second movement recalling a lyrical romance and, finally, the rushing cascade of melodies in the finale.*

All the same Khrennikov's new composition came under fire. The critics' complaints, predictably enough, included gratuitous accusations of an ill-defined thematism and fragmented narration, and charges of insufficient purity of style. One critic claimed, for instance: *The second theme of the first movement, for all its outward effectiveness, seems to fail to meet the requirements of really good taste. . .* (?!) Of course, the audience who liked the Concerto might well have objected that the critic seemed to be wrong on that point. But it was by now an established tradition among

Khrennikov and violinist Leonid Kogan. The close cooperation between the composer and the performer is in keeping with a time-honored tradition in Soviet music that includes such examples as Shostakovich and Yevgeni Mravinsky, or Prokofiev and Emil Gilels.

the critics to leave a "fly in the ointment" of their reviews of whatever Khrennikov wrote. And yet those who liked the Concerto were proved right as was U. Koriev who wrote in his detailed review: *The best of this Concerto is fully consonant with the spirit of the times and possesses everything to guarantee it a long life in the concert hall.*

And so it was. The Concerto epitomized the best features of Khrennikov's work and over the past quarter century brilliantly proved its viability, unlike many violin concertos written by other composers over the period. Apparently, this inspired Khrennikov to come back to this genre fifteen years later to produce a vivid and even more artistic second violin concerto. One of the crowning achievements of Khrennikov's entire career, it is also one of the best concertos of the twentieth century.

Leonid Kogan commented: *". . .I felt that writing music for violin on a large scale appealed to Tikhon Khrennikov and I was convinced that sooner or later he would return to the violin. And so he did. I remember how in the mid 70's he said to me: 'I'm working on my second violin concerto, if you are interested.' I was not a bit surprised. Later it was my good fortune and privilege to be the first violinist to play it and I am naturally proud that the composer has dedicated both of his violin concertos to me."*

The *Second Concerto* for violin and orchestra was one of the few of Khrennikov's compositions that received immediate critical acclaim without any reservations. Both the performers and audiences were delighted. Interestingly, the Concerto won its success despite its innovative and largely uncommon character which, as Leonid Kogan rightly observed, was antipodal to the *First Concerto*. Indeed, the *First Violin Concerto* is a traditional three-movement cycle opening with a Sonata

Yevgeny Svetlanov conducts as Leonid Kogan performs Tikhon Khrennikov's *Second Violin Concerto* in the Great Hall of the Conservatory. ". . .It was my good fortune and privilege to be the first violinist to play it."

The delegation of Soviet musicians after a tour in Czechoslovakia. Left to right: Emil Gilels and his wife, Tikhon and Klara Khrennikov, composer Marian Koval, Leonid Kogan with wife Elizaveta Gilels.

Allegro. Its dramatic design follows a familiar pattern: both the lyric Andante and the impetuous finale Rondo perform their usual functions. The dramatic design of the *Second Concerto* is rather unusual. A very brief and dynamic first movement in which the introductory monologue of the solo violin seems to provide an impetus to all subsequent development, is followed by the second movement which carries the bulk of the Concerto's emotional and semantic burden. Whereas the middle part of his *First Concerto* is of predominantly contemplative character, the enchantingly beautiful Andante of the *Second Concerto* is steeped in deep dramaticism which in terms of its emotional intensity is as powerful as any of the comparable pages of Prokofiev's scores. And only the finale of the *Second Concerto* is similar to that of the *First Concerto* in its pressure, boisterous gaiety and dance-like vividness. . . All this adds up to a rather unexpected but still integral cycle in terms of the inherent continuity of musical thought.

Understandably, Khrennikov's *Second Violin Concerto* was immediately included in the repertoire of the foremost violin virtuosos. Each of them interprets the Concerto in his own way, finding in it that which suits his individuality. We can gain a good idea of the enchanting quality of the *Second Violin Concerto* from the opinions of two foremost violinists, two of its best interpreters. **Grigori Zhislin:** *As a student I played Khrennikov's* First Violin Concerto *and I had the impression that he liked my interpretation. In any case soon after he had completed his* Second Concerto *he gave me the music and I had great pleasure in adding the Concerto to my repertoire. Over the past few years I have played this composition in many cities at home and abroad. I have also recorded a performance with the*

Moscow Philharmonic under Dmitri Kitayenko and I have played it on television supported by an orchestra conducted by Vladimir Fedoseyev... In short, the Second Concerto is very much a part of my repertoire. What appeals to me in it is its expressive musical language with a touch of purely Khrennikovian virtuosity. You feel that it's been written by a composer who is a brilliant performer himself with an intimate knowledge of various instruments, not just the piano. The Concerto is difficult but these are rewarding difficulties for the performer which enable him to display different facets of his skill (if any). Despite its limpid clarity and apparent simplicity, Khrennikov's music is very rich and colorful abounding in chromaticisms, exquisite modulations, purely instrumental shifts, emotional switchovers and changes of pace, double notes, chords and giddy, breathtaking passages. Besides, like the First Concerto, it demands from the performer a strong powerful sound, a full cantilena and mastery of a very full palette of sound colors, and maximum emotional intensity.

Khrennikov and Grigori Zhislin, one of the best interpreters of Khrennikov's *Second Violin Concerto*. "Whenever I play the Second Concerto I experience an uplift."

Whenever I play the Second Concerto I experience an uplift, for it demands of the performer a mobilization of his physical and spiritual powers, reminding him that the term 'virtuosity' is derived from 'virtue' meaning strength, manliness. And another thing, the Concerto *has an extremely vivid imagery. To give a correct interpretation to the resilient first movement with its pointed lack of a lyric theme, the performer should be capable in the course of the moto-like movement of the music to bring out the softer emotive current that runs through it. The second movement, to my mind, is the dramatic focal point of the* Concerto. *This is an inspired cantilena with its instantly recognizable Russian character, a cantilena that Khrennikov has such a complete command of whether in vocal or instrumental music. Witness the intensely dramatic climax of the* Concerto, *the amazingly broad flood of melody, and those enchantingly beautiful exchanges between strings and winds. Finally we come to the finale with its bold tonal comparisons, the fiery temperamental rhythm and impulsive unfolding of the material. The sparkling gaiety of the concluding section worthily crowns off the cycle which is a veritable paean in praise of life... Audience response has always been ecstatic wherever I played the* Concerto *whether in respectable, exclusive concert halls or in workmen's clubs at factories and plants.*

Violinist Igor Oistrakh (left), in whose repertoire music by Tikhon Khrennikov "has figured prominently . . . in recent years,' autographing a program of his recital for Vice President of Paganiniana Publications Gary Hersch.

Mikhail Khomitser, Tikhon Khrennikov, David Oistrakh and Igor Bezrodny (left to right) backstage after a concert in which M. Khomitser and I. Bezrodny played the cello and the violin solo parts and David Oistrakh was at the conductor's stand.

Igor Oistrakh. *The music of Tikhon Khrennikov has figured prominently in my performing repertoire in recent years. Our friendship and creative contacts date from the appearance of the* Second Violin Concerto. *I like it very much. It is noted for rich musical content and expresses the composer's thoughts most clearly. The* Concerto *contains not a single false note and its unusual form is extraordinarily interesting. I can hardly recall any other composition for violin with a similar aphoristically brief first movement. It is in the nature of an introduction to the narrative of the following two movements. The lyrical Adagio is exceptionally sincere and enchantingly elegant. The* Concerto's *theme, both plastic and exquisite with its elaborate and rich harmonic attire, is first treated by the clarinets before the violin takes over. Curiously enough, the violin is used here in the upper register for the most part with the result that its solo singing soars high in the sky. This is designed to emphasize the purity, radiance and sincerity of the music. The surging highly dramatic tutti are marvelous and the poetical conclusion touched with romantic pensiveness where the muted violin passages intermingle with the theme sustained by the oboe is deeply moving. A powerful, overwhelming, march-like finale written in a masterly temperamental manner comes as a sharp but justified contrast. The finale is difficult for the performer not only in technical terms but also because of the character of its musical material. The performer has the challenging task of conveying the composer's individual style which manifests itself both in its polytonality, in a vivid, "high-relief" melodic pattern and in the "high tension" of the movement. One other distinctive feature of the* Concerto's *form is the absence of the traditional cadenza. This is dictated by the compressed nature of the material; the violin part provides an extraordinarily wide scope for the soloist to display the full range of his skill. In short, what I mean is that the* Second Concerto *is one of my favorites in the modern violin repertoire."*

This is how two artists with widely different creative individualities assess Khrennikov's *Second Violin Concerto.* They interpret it differently

in accordance with their particular gift. It is difficult to say which interpretation the audiences enjoy more: the enchanting lyricism and concentration of Igor Oistrakh's treatment or the powerful sweep and sparkling virtuosity of Grigori Zhislin. There is no need to choose between the two. This music allows great scope for individual interpretation to bring out new facets of its beauty. . .

The birth of yet another of Khrennikov's compositions in recent years is associated with the name of Igor Oistrakh. We refer to the cycle of three pieces for violin and piano first performed at a festival held in the Estonian city of Parnu in 1978 commemorating David Oistrakh. Shortly afterward it was first played abroad in Austria at a traditional festival in Carinthia. Incidentally, the sponsors of the festival had commissioned this composition in the first place. Even at that time it was obvious that this opus, modestly entitled by the author, *The Three Pieces* (Dithyranl, Intermezzo, Dance) was an integrated cycle in terms of its dramatic design. That was precisely how H. Schneider, one of Austria's foremost music scholars, saw it: *As for the* Three Pieces *for violin and piano they are essentially a three-part sonata, pure and simple, whose music has an enchanting virtuoso quality in the first and third movements which frame the very sensuous cantilena Intermezzo.* The sonata character of the work is also emphasized by the fact that its piano part is not second to the violin part in terms of significance, richness of texture and virtuosity. Igor Oistrakh has commented: *In this respect Khrennikov's composition, to my mind, can be ranked with such celebrated works for violin as Prokofiev's* Five Melodies *or Szymanowski's* Myths *cycle.*

Tikhon Khrennikov performing his *Second Piano Concerto* for the workers of the Likhachov Automobile Plant. ". . .A life-affirming composition designed to put the listener in an optimistic frame of mind and make him feel the joy of being a member of the human race. . ."

It was precisely the cyclic completeness and richness of the piano texture that led Khrennikov to transcribe the *Three Pieces* for orchestra thereby converting it into something of a concertino. Since then Khrennikov's *Three Pieces* has often been performed by chamber and symphony orchestras. Its concluding *Dance* section was also included in the repertoire of the VII International Tchaikovsky Competition. Curiously enough, by no means did all the contestants who played it cope with this apparently unpretentious piece. Most of them failed to bring out its complex polytonal structure and its elaborate rhythmic pattern. This test proved once again that Khrennikovian simplicity implies far more than meets the eye.

For all the diversity of opinions of the character of Khrennikov's talent, on one point nit-picking critics, enthusiastic performers and ordinary music lovers, are in agreement, and that is that the beauty and natural tunefulness of thematism constitute a priceless quality of the composer's talent which no one can deny. And it was entirely logical that the composer should later turn to the cello, that immemorially cantilena instrument. Soon after the première of his *First Violin Concerto* Khrennikov thought of writing a concerto for cello and orchestra. Although he first mentioned his intention in 1960, the idea did not come to fruition until four years later.

It seemed that the essential harmony between Khrennikov's melodic gift and the character of the cello would predetermine a traditional enough treatment, with no surprises. Actually, however, the treatment was anything but traditional. While not violating the melodious song-like nature of the cello, the composer displayed considerable fantasy both in his handling of the instrument's expressive possibilities and in his approach to the dramaticism of the cello concerto as a genre. The *Concerto's* form was rather unusual coming after its predecessor—the *First Violin Concerto*. The structure of the new composition was also original: the two first movements—Prelude, and Aria—were in slow tempo while the *Concerto* ended in a dynamic Sonata. The content of each movement was

Khrennikov receiving the President of the International Music Council, Frank Callaway (Australia). 1981.

unorthodox. Inherent in the unhurried Prelude with its sensitive contemplative mood is a considerable power and drive. The exchanges between the solo cello and the bassoon, the flute, the viola, the glockenspiel and the first violin, seem to give a foretaste of the events about to unfold. The overall character of the music does not change in the poetic contemplative "Aria" (yet another admirable example of Khrennikov's adagios). However, because of the compression of the musical material the two movements do not create an impression of bleak monotony. Each in its own way prepares the audience for the dramatic flare-up of the Sonata-Allegro finale. The stark contrast between the pensive, serene placid music of the first two movements and the whirlwind of the Sonata is breathtaking in its overwhelming impact.

The *Cello Concerto* embodied Khrennikov's desire to take a fresh look at the constructive possibilities of the concerto cycle (a desire he first exhibited while still a student at the Moscow Conservatory). Against this background the conclusion drawn by one musicologist about allegedly by "ancient sources of the composition" merely on the strength of the names and the order of the movements seems pretty far-fetched. On the contrary, this shows a conscious desire to intensify the form, to make it more dynamic by ignoring, overcoming the orthodox concerto framework. As always in Khrennikov's case these quests are dictated not by a yen for cheap surface effects but by a deep-felt need for maximum self-expression, need to express his world outlook in a straightforward, accessible language. Therefore, although appearing in new dress, the composer remains essentially himself. Rodion Shchedrin noted this in his comment soon after the Cello Concerto's first public performance: *Its appeal*

Tikhon Khrennikov has worked tirelessly to maintain and enhance the worldwide status of Soviet music. Here he is shown with two great fellow composers, Dmitri Shostakovich and Dmitri Kabalevsky, at a press conference in Los Angeles.

derives from the Concerto's radiant lyrical tone and candid feelings and its soft pastel colors. It seems to me that this music glows with a kind smile and sings a pleasant pensive song while the boisterous dance defines the range of its imagery and emotionality.

For over fifteen years now Mikhail Khomitser has been one of the best interpreters of the Cello Concerto. He recalls: *I began learning this composition more or less as soon as Tikhon Nikolayevich completed its first movement. I was thus able to check with the composer my reactions and impressions. That was, of course, a fairly long time ago. Since then I have played the* Concerto *so often that frankly I have lost count. Of the many performances, the one I gave at a traditional music festival in the Bulgarian city of Rusa was perhaps the most memorable. On that occasion I performed the cello concertos of Shostakovich and Khrennikov on the same program, in the presence of the composers. I remember how warmly Shostakovich praised Khrennikov's concerto. I also felt flattered.*

Indeed, Khrennikov's Cello Concerto *is an altogether captivating piece for performer and listener alike. Its powerful music may be likened to a compressed mainspring. In terms of logic of musical development and proportions, it reminds me of a perfect sculpture with everything superfluous neatly cut away by the master sculptor. This is particularly true of the first movement which is without question one of the peaks of Khrennikov's instrumental music. It captivates the listener with the infinite range and scope of its melodic breadth and equally with the lofty human feelings it expresses so well. What the performer finds particularly difficult is to soar to this dizzy height without any run-up, as it were. I can hardly recall any other cello concerto with a similarly unusual opening, only in Myaskovsky, perhaps. Besides,*

On Tikhon Khrennikov's 60th birthday, members of the younger generation of Soviet musicians came to wish him well. Left to right: pianist Yevgeni Mogilevsky, violinist Pavel Kogan, cellist Mikhail Khomitser (one of the best interpreters of Khrennikov's *Cello Concerto*), Tikhon Khrennikov, violinist Igor Bezrodny, pianists Nina Kogan and Vladimir Feltzman.

this part of the concerto displays brilliant instrumentation and an extra-ordinarily subtle duet treatment.

Khrennikov's Cello Concerto *(I may be partial, of course) epitomizes the distinctive features of the composer's musical world. While the first movement is brimful of lofty emotionality, the second movement is notable for its earthy, tangible beauty. Not surprisingly, the full and graphic sound of its "Aria" recalls operatic arias and its powerful climax demands from the soloist a fullness of cello sound akin to the human voice. The finale is one sparkling torrent of life-giving radiance, sunshine. . . At first sight the purely virtuoso passages carry a tremendous charge of feeling that affects the first two movements by its contrast with particular force. In short, the Concerto is a welcome challenge for the performer. It is his chance to shine.*

Unlike his violin concertos, Khrennikov's *Cello Concerto* did not immediately conquer the concert stage. It was only gradually that the cellists discovered its rich world and potential that was screened from view by the *Concerto's* rather unusual form. But since about the latter half of the 1970s, the *Cello Concerto* has been performed with increasing frequency both in this country and abroad. Its best interpreters include, apart from Khomitser, Valentin Feigin and Victoria Yagling.

A few years ago Khrennikov said: *As soon as I finish the ballet (he was referring to* The Hussar Ballad*) I will resume work on my* Second Concerto *for cello and orchestra. So far I have written two piano concertos, two violin concertos and only one for cello. I think I owe the cello a second concerto. You know, over a long period of time composers may radically change their attitude to a particular instrument and its possibilities. So in this composition I would like to express what I think of the cello now and how I feel it. I would like very much to emphasize its inexhaustible "singing" potential. And I intend to write my* Cello Concerto *in such a way as to ensure the dominance of the instrument's melodic generosity.*

Over the past ten years or so both the violin and the cello have been very much in the focus of Khrennikov's attention. And what of the piano?

Mikhail Khomitser. For over fifteen years now, he has included Khrennikov's *Cello Concerto* in his repetoire: ". . .An altogether captivating piece for performer and listener alike."

Well, the piano has been and remains by far his favorite instrument, even though during the past decade there were periods when it was rather neglected. Khrennikov's burst of creativity during these years produced one score after another in a variety of genres. First he was distracted from the piano by his work on a children's opera, *The Boy Giant*, commissioned by the Children's Theatre directed by Natalia Satz. It seemed at first that this opera would not require too much effort considering the nature of the audience. Actually, however, Khrennikov got so carried away that he decided to write a fairy-tale opera with a full-scale plot packed with vivid vocal, instrumental and dance episodes. *The Boy Giant* was a resounding success both in Moscow and in other cities.

That was yet another example of Khrennikov's "forays" into a new genre. Unfortunately, there was no follow-up. In the meantime, Khrennikov's piano recitals were becoming more frequent and invariably satisfying for him. Khrennikov often said in the mid-60s: *"Of course, the composer's chief business is to write music, but I find it sometimes very difficult to resist the temptation to perform my own compositions. Unfortunately I do not have enough time for piano practice. Even so I try to do what I can to keep my hand in and that is why I regularly accept invitations to play my* Piano Concerto *in different cities at home and abroad. These recitals help me to keep my performing flair intact and this does no harm to my composing. True, mine is a composer's pianism, but I am glad to see that the audiences accept it.*

A scene from *The Boy Giant*.

Perhaps he was being too modest there. The solid foundation of Khrennikov's "composer's" pianism, for which he tends to apologize, was

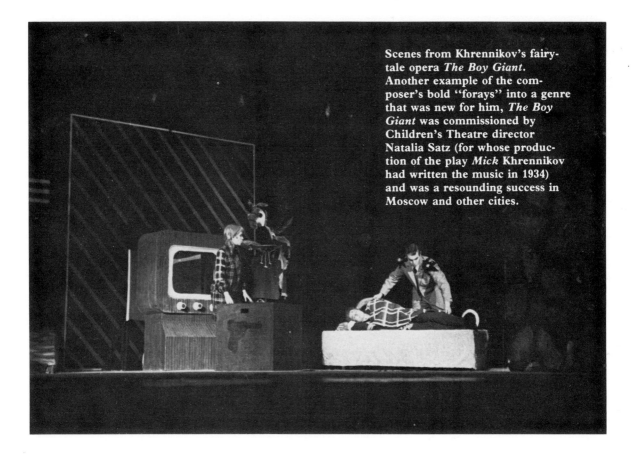

Scenes from Khrennikov's fairy-tale opera *The Boy Giant*. Another example of the composer's bold "forays" into a genre that was new for him, *The Boy Giant* was commissioned by Children's Theatre director Natalia Satz (for whose production of the play *Mick* Khrennikov had written the music in 1934) and was a resounding success in Moscow and other cities.

laid during his years at the Moscow Conservatory where he attained a professional level as a pianist. This professionalism did not wear off with the years.

Incidentally, here, too, tradition has had an important part to play. Taneyev, Rachmaninoff, Scriabin, Prokofiev and Shostakovich were all superlative pianists and, perhaps, the best performers of their own compositions. Despite his incredibly tight schedule, Khrennikov stoutly refused to give up his piano playing, seeing it as an organic component of his work as a composer. Hardly anyone would surpass him in the interpretation of his own piano compositions. Their character and spirit harmonize so well with his own character and the spirit of his piano technique. Leonid Kogan the violinist once made this rather puzzled comment: *I don't quite see how, with little more than snatched moments for piano practice, he can still play as well as he does. The impression you get is that he creates music right there on stage, telling its tale with his hands. Indeed, this "composer's" pianism compares favorably with the polished performance of many a professional pianist on account of its improvised brilliance and immediacy, its naturalness of expression. I fully agree with B. Pokrovski, who says that Khrennikov's music-making captivates you, infecting you with an amazing surge of emotion, organic fullness of sound and great intensity of feeling.*

It was entirely logical, therefore, that his irresistable urge to play his own compositions before concert hall audiences should have prompted Khrennikov to add a new piano concerto to his performing repertory. This concerto, his second, conceived in the early 1960s was completed in the autumn of 1971. On the day of its first performance, February 8, 1972 Khrennikov told his friends: *"I feel terribly excited. Though rather*

Leonid Kogan performing.

In the Great Hall of the Moscow Conservatory, Tikhon Khrennikov performs his *Second Piano Concerto*—**written "in such a way as to enable the pianist to display the full range of his technical brilliance."**

Tikhon Khrennikov, the pianist. ". . .I find it sometimes very difficult to resist the temptation to perform my own compositions."

difficult to perform, my Second Concerto *is fully in line with my policy of writing for piano in such a way as to enable the pianist to display the full range of his technical brilliance. I wrote it with this in mind."*

On the content of his new composition, Khrennikov was rather laconic: My Second Piano Concerto *was conceived as a life-affirming composition designed to put the listener in an optimistic frame of mind and make him feel the joy of being a member of the human race on this beautiful home planet of ours, of being able to create. I also wanted it to be pleasant and to enable the pianist to test his virtuoso potential. I wanted to take a fresh look at this form and to overcome its standard. The Concerto is in three movements to be played without interruption. The slow first movement—a piano cadenza with an orchestral contribution towards the end; the second movement in fast tempo is a kind of follow-up to the first; the third is a finale with a major piano cadenza in the middle of it.*

This rather lapidary annotation does not do justice to the concerto's content nor does it give an idea of its place in Khrennikov's work. And this place is important as the *Second Piano Concerto* and the *Third Symphony* that followed it were in many ways the focal points of the innovative quests of a mature master, refracted through the prism of his idiosyncratic talent. Let us hear what the musician who, together with the composer, was the first to perform this composition has to say about it. He is Yevgeny Svetlanov, conductor and composer.

What is the new element that the score of this composition contains? writes Svetlanov. *In broad outline it is this: a broadly conceived, dominating and masterly solo part. Actually the whole of the first movement is a major solo piano episode which opens with a modest one-voice exposition of the first theme and is followed up by a polyphonic development of the musical*

The composer in his country home, at work on the *Second Piano Concerto*. The Concerto, "an outstanding phenomenon of Soviet musical life," scored many triumphs in the cities of the Soviet Union as well as abroad.

Yevgeny Svetlanov conducts as Tikhon Khrennikov performs the *Second Piano Concerto* in the Great Hall of the Conservatory. "The impression you get is that he creates music right there on stage, telling its tale with his hands."

material. As new voices are introduced the polyphonic structure becomes more complicated as new piano registers gradually come into play and the whole builds up to a tremendous avalanche of sound. The climax of this episode is completed by a highly expressive contribution from the strings and then the whole orchestra joins in a brilliant C-Major with a persistently repeated D-Flat in the high register. This episode will recur at the end of the composition thereby forming a kind of musical arch, gradually dying down with a persistently repeated bell-like sound in the same D-Flat against the background of a fading orchestra and piano.

The second movement, Sonata, follows without a break. Its music is extremely dynamic, full of explosive power, octave cascades and exchanges between orchestra and piano. In this movement the solo piano and the orchestra are equally important. In fact, they are in competition with each other. Only in the middle of the second movement does a new musical image, very typical of Khrennikov's music with its touch of gentle humor, appear in the orchestra and is later taken up by the piano. In this movement we again hear a broad piano cadenza. Extremely rich and varied, this cadenza, written in a virtuoso style, leads to a reprise. The second movement ends in a dynamic, aggressive finish which creates the impression that it is the finale of the whole composition. But it isn't.

The third movement begins. Here the composer, instead of providing sharply contrasting material took the line of . . . maximum resistance, so to speak. Instead of a slow and contrasting passage, as expected, Khrennikov provides a boisterous and rhythmically resilient Rondo, full of humor. The tempo of this section is moderately restrained. The crisp theme with the recurrent first *four sounds against the background of a surging orchestral accompaniment captivates the listener straight from the opening bars. The whole of the finale is built along these lines in the middle of which the piano part is again assigned a fairly broad, polyphonically saturated, masterly cadenza. As a result of the finale's development, the composer returns to the music that concludes the first movement. This treatment of the cycle is original, if somewhat unexpected. Nonetheless, the form of the composition has been calculated with great precision and considerable conviction. It conveys very well the composer's unerring sense of the whole, his sense of proportion as between the movements and within each. And the more you listen to this concerto the more you appreciate the organic nature of its concept put forward by the composer.*

This analytical profile of the *Concerto* conveys the impressions of an eminent musician as accurately and fully as words can express it. Here we have an artist commenting on the work of a fellow artist. It is difficult to add anything worthwhile to Svetlanov's description. Perhaps we should emphasize yet again the remarkable, dual-unity of the impulses that gave rise to this concerto. On the one hand, it marks the pinnacle of the composer's mature thought, intellectual concentration and conscious rationality in his approach to the material, its selection and arrangement, of his philosophical insight and an ability to get a bird's-eye view of the whole at a glance, as it were. On the other hand, the *Concerto* is full of youthful freshness, indicating the as yet unspent reserves of the composer's spiritual youth . . . This is no exaggeration and not a few critics have pointed it out in the context of Khrennikov's later compositions. But often these critics and some musicians have ungraciously implied that Khrennikov's "spiritual youth" smacks of infantilism, belated naivete and attempts to recapture his own youth. But is it not, in this context, a hundred times more important that Khrennikov has a largely unspent ability for self-renovation? He has a flair for new ideas in life and

Khrennikov with British composer Benjamin Britten in Moscow.

Khrennikov after the performance of his *Third Symphony*, with one of its best interpreters, conductor Vladimir Fedoseyev.

in art, and an extraordinary sense of the present. The *Second Concerto* is ample proof of this. It is hard to say which of these two aspects of his creative personality surprised, and even puzzled, the critics more, critics who had long grown accustomed to pinning stereotyped labels on Khrennikov's compositions. It can safely be said that it was precisely a happy combination of these qualities that convinced and captivated the performers. That is why within a few years the *Second Piano Concerto* has joined the big league of the world's best piano works alongside the masterpieces of Prokofiev whose traditions Khrennikov has carried on so well. Once again let us hear from a performer. It is always worth listening to a performer as he can always be depended upon to say something very subjective, in the good sense of the term. Indeed, a performing artist normally includes a new composition in his repertory for the impeccable reason that he likes it. He knows its merits and tries to put them across to the audience and, most importantly, his anticipation of audience response is usually unmistakable. Here is what Nikolai Petrov, a pianist of note, has to say: *I have been fortunate to perform Khrennikov's* First Piano Concerto *on many occasions and I can testify that each time it was most enthusiastically received. Soviet and foreign audiences were even more ecstatic about his* Second Piano Concerto. *I witnessed the triumph Khrennikov scored after his own performance of the* Second Concerto *in a series of piano recitals in Spain. I have played this Concerto in Moscow, Leningrad, Saratov, Kishinyov, Kuibyshev and elsewhere in the Soviet Union with the country's best symphony orchestras and I must say that each time I discover new facets, new colors and new expressive nuances in it. This highly evocative music seems to epitomize the world of ideas of an intelligent and original ar-*

149

tist who sees in the world we live in not only its ugly conflicts, not only the seamy side of life but also beautiful things which make our lives worth living . . . Khrennikov's Second Piano Concerto *is without doubt an outstanding phenomenon of Soviet musical life. Its exact and fresh colors, its excellent pianism and brilliant orchestration combine to assure for the* Concerto *a leading place in today's piano repertory. A searching, forward-looking composer, Khrennikov while staying within the mainstream of the best traditions of world pianism often strikes out in new directions, following untrodden paths and finding new forms and artistically convincing means of musical expression.*

Soon after the *Second Piano Concerto,* Khrennikov completed his *Third Symphony,* which reflected his artistic credo at a new phase of his evolution. Although the scores of the *Second Concerto* and *Third Symphony* have much in common: grand scale, concentrated expression of the dominant ideas, an original interpretation of form and instrumental colors, their genre distinctions are manifest. Unlike many of today's composers who tend to turn an instrumental concerto into something of a symphony with a solo instrument, Khrennikov has remained loyal to the classical interpretation of the genre as being strictly dialogue-based. As for the symphony, for Khrennikov, as for his great predecessors and contemporaries, it has been and remains one of the principal forms of musical comment on specific issues of the day or on perennial problems of human existence. This rather traditional attitude does not preclude a fresh approach to a particular treatment of the construction of the symphonic cycle. Several years before the appearance of the *Third Symphony,* Khrennikov said: *Some people took the view that the golden age of the symphony came to an end somewhere at the turn of the century with the demise of the leading lights of Russian and West European music. Fortunately, these theorists have been proved wrong. The symphony lives on and has been brilliantly developed in the twentieth century by brilliant masters. Suffice it to name only Soviet musicians: Myaskovski, Prokofiev and Shostakovich who have made an invaluable contribution to the development of this genre.*

We should add to this list many foreign composers. The symphony is very much alive, it is living music which is needed by music lovers as much as ever it was. This is a genre which enables the composer to express vividly, and in a large way, what he thinks of life, his commentary on the passing scene and to reveal his own inner world. At the same time the symphony is constantly evolving, acquiring new features depending on the times and the individuality of the composer.

The *Third Symphony*, whose idea took a long time to take shape and mature, is a good illustration of Khrennikov's creative credo. Although it has no program character, its themes are inspired by the topical issues of today's world.

The *Third Symphony* had its first public performance on March 11, 1974 in the Grand Hall of the Moscow Conservatory. The State Symphony Orchestra of the USSR was conducted by Yevgeny Svetlanov. Many who were there that evening probably remember the atmosphere of uplift which reigned at the Grand Hall and the standing ovation which the audience gave the performers. This ovation caused some confusion among the specialists for what they heard was a score with a rare transparency of sound, unusual form and compressed character of musical thought.

Indeed, in his *Third Symphony*, Khrennikov who had by then turned sixty, had abandoned many of the generally accepted canons. Instead of the usual Sonata Allegro, the first movement was a rushing, impetuous Fugue brimful of imaginative thematic comparisons and juxtapositions, polyphonic developments and irrepressible movement. And the whole of this vivid figurative kaleidoscope of images lasts for a fleeting three minutes. The audience is under the impression that this is some kind of prologue which captures the imagination with its dazzling richness of color, the impetuous thrust of movement and the sparkling interplay of instrumental timbres. This torrent inevitably involves audience consciousness; it intrigues the audience, forcing them to hold their breath as they await the unfolding of further events. These events also develop in

Khrennikov and outstanding French composer Andre Jolivet are bound by the ties of an old friendship.

the lyrical Andante-Sostenuto (second movement) and in the Finale (Allegro con Fuoco). Different critics react differently to the dramatic significance of these movements. Some believe that the middle section with its exalted lyricism, enchanting serene flood of melody, its powerful dramatic climax, carries the bulk of the semantic burden. Others take the view that the symphony's center of gravity resides in its Finale—the apotheosis celebrating the indestructible joy of living, a full-blooded attitude to the world around us. We believe that the composer has provided more grounds for different conclusions. On close scrutiny and on listening to the symphony in performance, its dramatic construction comes over in indissoluble unity and complete integrity. This is seen, for instance, both in the polyphonic exchanges between the Fugue and the finale, and the interconnection of the lyrical images in the intermezzo and the middle episode of the third movement (Largo), and also in the symbolic return in the finale of the "motive of time"—the clock rhythm provided by the harps and the bells earlier in the Intermezzo. It should be added that, while finding new constructive solutions and means of expression, Khrennikov remains himself both in characteristic thematic turns of phrase which grow into an extensive cantilena, and in rhythmic structures, now playful, now crisp and precise, and also in the winsome, typically Khrennikovian brio. In this sense, the *Third Symphony* is the product of a master made wise by the experience of decades of life and steady effort. It inevitably brings back memories of the *First Symphony*, the first major achievement of his career. Significantly, Khrennikov dedicated his *Third Symphony* to Heinrich Litinsky, one of his teachers at the Conservatory.

Vladimir Fedoseyev, the conductor, one of the best interpreters of the work, has said: *The Third Symphony epitomizes that which is perhaps the most important and valuable in Tikhon Khrennikov's work. The chief merit of this composition, as I see it, is the profound idea implicit in it and expressed by melodic means. This unity of melody and idea, which is so much a feature of Khrennikov's work generally, is strongly felt in the symphony. Also manifest are its deep national roots. But this does not limit the symphony's universal appeal and it invariably brings an appreciative response from audiences both at home and abroad. This symphony is also a reflection of the human soul, a mirroring of today's world with the throbbing and uneasy pulse of its life. Khrennikov's music has a light tonality and is always optimistic. The supreme purpose of art has always been to elevate and celebrate man, and the optimism and the triumph of good that Khrennikov's music conveys serve this lofty purpose well. This is not to say that his music is devoid of dramatic and even tragic overtones, but in the end, the world of light invariably triumphs over darkness.*

I believe modern man needs a sense of harmony badly. This sense of harmony is often sadly lacking in the world around us and that has been responsible for many conflicts in today's world. Unfortunately, there is much in contemporary art that does not help people find a way out of the impasse. To be sure, search and exploration are always important and in fact essential but, surely, the purpose of the search and its direction are vital. This sense of purpose and direction characterizes Khrennikov's quest which returns us, in a new dimension, to the great classical values of beauty and harmony.

The third movement of the symphony contains an episode in which the

Tikhon Khrennikov.

mechanistic character of the movement seems to come into sharp conflict with the melody and then this movement, the wheel of life which seems to be spinning with inexorable force, suddenly stops to admire the beautiful sound of the trombone.

The *Third Symphony,* thus, is a kind of quintessence of Khrennikov's philosophy as an artist. Much has been written about it, with different analysts giving different interpretations to its imagery and content. We hesitate to follow in the wake of these analysts and try to find verbal equivalents for the rich multi-faceted musical substance of the *Third Symphony* which the composer himself describes as *the result of my reflections over many years on the meaning of life, and the place of man in today's world.* And in any case this is not a particularly rewarding occupation as one is apt to slip into unjustified generalizations prompted by subjective perceptions. We believe that any attempt at this is bound to be a rather far-fetched strained interpretation. But if there is one readily identifiable image in the score, it is perhaps the image of a symbolic clock that ticks confidently on . . . This symphony is about our time.

Khrennikov's music has been a permanent item in the concert hall repertory for decades now. His major compositions have been performed by some of the nation's best symphony orchestras and soloists. The composer's musical evenings have long become a regular feature of the concert season. On such occasions, apart from symphonies and instrumental concertos, Khrennikov's romances, vocal cycles and excerpts from his operas are performed. The composer's piano recitals are always enthusiastically received by the audiences. Concerts featuring Khrennikov's works are often held in huge auditoriums seating thousands and invariably draw capacity audiences.

Interest in Khrennikov's music has been steadily growing outside his native country. Over the past two years he has appeared as a performing pianist in practically every major cultural central in Europe, the Americas and Asia. Here is a short run-down of the major highlights of the triumphant march of his music across the world:

1959—the *First Symphony* is performed in New York, Boston and Philadelphia in the composer's presence, Charles Munch and Eugene Ormandy conducting.

1961—the *Second Symphony* and the *Violin Concerto* (Igor Bezrodny) are performed at the International Festival of Modern Music in Los Angeles. The conductor was Franz Waxman.

1963—Tikhon Khrennikov makes his debut as a soloist on tour abroad performing his *First Piano Concerto* in Dresden, Leipzig, Berlin, and Weimar.

1964—a series of concerts given by the composer in Bulgaria. Dobrin Petkov conducted. Khrennikov's compositions were also performed by Nikolai Gyuzelev, Ioko Sato, Valentin Feigin and the composer himself.

The composer with Franz Waxman, who conducted his *Second Symphony* and *First Violin Concerto* at the International Festival of Modern Music in Los Angeles, in 1961.

Top: Tikhon Khrennikov with children's writer Sergei Mikhalkov and Japanese violinist Ioko Sato, who performed the composer's works in Bulgaria in 1964. Bottom: Tikhon Khrennikov signing the Cooperation Agreement with the British Music Council.

1965 – a month-long tour of Japan during which Khrennikov performed his compositions for the piano in the mammoth concert halls of Tokyo, Osaka, and Kyoto.

1966 – a tour of Paris and Bordeaux. The composer performs his *Piano Concerto* with the ORTF orchestra (of the French Radio and Television) under Charles Bruck. The Lamoureux Orchestra performs the *First Symphony*. Jacques Oatman conducted.

1973 – Khrennikov took part in a festival of Soviet music in Britain.

1974 – Khrennikov makes his debut in Rome's Auditorium Hall of the Accademia Nazionale di Santa Cecilia. For three consecutive days the composer performed his *Second Piano Concerto*.

1976 – Khrennikov gives piano recitals in Philadelphia and in Italy.

1978 – a series of concerts devoted to Khrennikov's work are given as part of the traditional festival in Carinthia Austria.

1983 – Khrennikov *Third Symphony* performed by the N.J. State Orchestra under Murray Glass.

The list is long . . . To complete it we would have to mention hundreds of concerts given over the years in Czechoslovakia, Romania, the GDR, Bulgaria, Yugoslavia, Spain, Norway, Finland, West Germany, Poland, Hungary, and other countries where the composer either appeared in piano recitals or where his music was played. . .

What is it about Khrennikov's music that appeals so much to audiences everywhere? What is it that has assured for it such a conspicuous place in the panorama of contemporary music? Like any major artistic phenomenon of true worth, Khrennikov's art possesses a series of qualities and

dimensions which in their totality have assured for it a unique place among the musical achievements of the twentieth century.

. . .Speaking of the work of his friend Georges Auric, the outstanding French composer, Khrennikov once made this remarkable comment: *I see Auric's adherence to high principles above all in his unswerving loyalty to the great classical traditions. He has never betrayed these traditions either in his own work as a composer or in his truly titanic activity as a public man. Auric goes by living human perception and takes into account the artistic tastes of the mass of the public. I see Auric's adherence to high principles also in his unchanging orientation towards the national expressiveness of art, in his permanent interest in the sources of the cultural heritage of the French people. I see Auric's adherence to high principles in the wide range of his work. We all know that Sergei Diaghilev staged the ballets of the young Auric in Paris but few know that Auric has also written one of the most popular waltzes in France as part of his music score for a film.* The same fully applies to Khrennikov himself not only because these words reflect his firm esthetic position but also because they are true of his own work which has grown up on a different national soil and blossomed under different social conditions.

These words bring us back to the sources of Khrennikov's work. We have already dealt at some length with its early connections with various strata of the Russian folk song tradition, with his attachment to the urban folklore which has often incurred the "righteous" wrath of the purists within the critical fraternity. It is also pertinent and important to mention one more side to his creative genesis, namely, those towering figures of the past and present who influenced the making of his artistic personality. One of Khrennikov's biographers, U. Kremliev, has put together a pretty comprehensive list of influences that Khrennikov has, according to Kremliev, been subject to: Bach, Schubert, Glinka, Mussorgsky, Rimsky-Korsakov, Tchaikovsky, Scriabin, Wagner, Bizet, Debussy, Ravel, Berg, Hindemith, Stravinsky, Prokofiev, Shostakovich, and Blanter. And this list could be continued if we leaf through other books and other articles, to eventually have a sort of synopsis of the history of music. Apparently the work of any twentieth century composer contains one or another intonational turn of phrase, a constructive device, a harmonic combination which will remind us of at least one of the composers mentioned above. There is hardly any need to prove that any artist absorbs the sum total of the experience of his predecessors, both distant and more immediate. But at the same time the roots of the work of a major composer reach deep.

As regards permanent artistic models and benchmarks in Khrennikov's case these are, above all, Bach, Tchaikovsky and Prokofiev. The musical ideas of these titans representing three different centuries have fertilized Khrennikov's creative fantasy and are refracted in his individual character and style. What remains unchanged is his penchant for the polyphonic methods of development, for horizontal structures in their movement (here the arc clearly stretches from his *First Piano Concerto* to the *Second Concerto*, more specifically, to its famous introduction based on the twelve-tone scale). But this is not the main thing that attracts Khrennikov to Bach. The main thing is the vibrant vitality of Bach's musical texture and the full-bloodedness of his music. And in this context we may

Top: Sergei Diaghilev. Bottom: Alban Berg, author of *Wozzek*, one of the many foreign composers whose influence Khrennikov absorbed into his own artistic experience.

Unique and original as it is, Khrennikov's work continues the great tradition of 19th Century classical Russian music. This picture of Khrennikov in the Glinka Museum of Smolensk, under the portrait of great Russian composer Mikhail Glinka, is almost symbolic of the tie.

marvel at the way the enthusiastic words spoken by Khrennikov during his student years (we quoted them in one of the first chapters) were echoed by a comment he made in 1974 when he said: *What captivates a person when he hears music? It is above all its emotionality, the way it touches the invisible chords of the human soul. Bach's music has this effect. That is why it moved his contemporaries and why it moves us. That is why it will continue to move succeeding generations of men. Many people ask themselves what is modern music? Paradoxical as it may sound, much of what is being written today may not be modern at all but what Bach wrote is very modern, even though he lived over two centuries ago.*

Far more obvious and direct are the links between Khrennikov and Prokofiev, that classic of the twentieth century. These links present a complex pattern and they manifest themselves in different ways in the composer's earlier works. The creative methods of the two composers, as we mentioned earlier on, coincide at many points in their opera scores of the 1930s—1940s. Khrennikov developed Prokofiev's traditions with great conviction in the instrumental music of a more mature period of his career. The main thing that these two artists have in common is the cheerfulness of their world outlook, the spontaneity of feeling which suggests the lightness of touch that characterized the creative approaches of both. The impetuous tempo of Khrennikov's scherzos, the toccata motor-like drive (the finale of the *Second Piano Concerto*), the infinite beauty of the Russian cantilena (exemplified by the Moderato from the *Second Violin Concerto*, among other things), the fantastic and, at times, grotesque imagery, of many pages of Khrennikov's music, all testify to the common artistic aspirations of Khrennikov and Prokofiev, aspirations which are perhaps the best examples in all of modern music of sound principles and faith in the beautiful. In this context Khrennikov's own words spoken quite recently are significant: *To this day two names are my favorites—Bach and Prokofiev. At first sight, their creative individualities seem to be antithetical. But in my mind they live in special harmony. Bach is the greatest and most enduring basis of the philosophic and polyphonic art of music. Prokofiev is a giant of the twentieth century who has opened up new horizons in music and has become a natural successor to the tradition of the great Russian classics. These two composers form the creative soil which nourishes the roots of my own work.*

To these great names Khrennikov always adds one more—Tchaikovsky. Over forty years ago he wrote: *Tchaikovsky is our great teacher. The scores of his symphonies, operas and ballets, the pages of his romances and compositions for chamber ensembles add up to the best textbook of compositional skill. We should all learn from Tchaikovsky how to approach creatively the rich heritage of folk songs. Witness the finales of his* Second *and* Fourth Symphonies, *his violin and piano concertos. With what brilliance does he transform folk songs into symphonic compositions. Tchaikovsky's operas in terms of their powerful dramaticism and depth of psychological treatment are unrivalled in the history of Russian music. Like no other Russian composer, Tchaikovsky had a genius for revealing the inner world of man.*

Indeed, Khrennikov has always sought to develop the Tchaikovskian traditions of natural musical utterance from heart to heart, a tradition which puts above all else the portrayal of genuine human feelings and movements of the soul. These are, in our opinion, the deep roots of Khrennikov's muse. But it is obvious that life itself with its kaleidoscope

Johann Sebastian Bach, one of Tikhon Khrennikov's lifelong idols. "Bach's soul is the soul of a human colossus who sees the seamy side of human affairs and expresses them in the language of his great art. Bach's music is an exploration of the real world of man as it is with everything that is evil and good in it."

Tikhon Khrennikov with one of the greatest masters of this century, Sergei Prokofiev. There are many complex yet direct links between the works of the two. To Khrennikov, Prokofiev is "a giant of the twentieth century who has opened up new horizons in music. . ."

of events and accelerating tempo has always provided rich food for thought and stimulated his imagination. Proof of this is supplied by the cardinal milestones of his work. These include his stage trilogy dealing with the revolutionary storms of the twentieth century, orchestral scores, songs and music for films and TV plays. A contemporary spirit in the broad sense of the term informs every aspect of Khrennikov's work—the choice of theme, plot, viewpoint and artistic means of expression. Khrennikov emphasizes: *The artist needs contemporary themes as much as he needs the air he breathes. Without maintaining a living bond with reality art would cease to exist . . . The notion of a contemporary theme should not be confined to current or recent events alone. The modern ring of a work of art is less a matter of the chronology of its theme and subject than a matter of the depth of treatment and of crisp portrayal of the spirit of the times. Of great importance here is the author's dominant idea and artistic concept, the way he depicts events and the people behind them and the message of his work. The artist may reflect events unfolding before his very eyes and yet, if his treatment is shallow and light-hearted, the contemporary spirit of his work turns out to be but a shabby imitation.* This last phrase helps us understand why Khrennikov has never written compositions calculated to score a one-day success, compositions which substitute a declamatory topicality for genuine sound musical content and message. The modern spirit of Khrennikov's works lies in the palpable authenticity of each of his characters. It lies in his ability to speak of the advanced ideas of our time in an adequate and consonant musical language.

A salient feature of the Khrennikovian style which could be said to symbolize our times to a certain extent is the unmistakable tenor of its ex-

pressive means. In this context the idea expressed by composer Andrei Petrov a few years ago seems to be relevant. He said: *Many people seem to think that the distinctly Soviet sound exists only in songs. I believe it is present both in symphonic and chamber music as well. Many of Khrennikov's scores are proof of that. They are dominated by an unmistakable Soviet flavor. I think we can safely speak of a particular intonational associative scale, a chain of intonations, echoes, semantic overtones which in their totality constitute a definite figurative structure which is associated in our minds with the image projected by the Soviet man of today.*

These true words shed light on one fairly widespread misconception about the distinctive features of Khrennikov's compositional style. We are referring to the persistent efforts of Khrennikov's detractors to detect in whatever he writes elements of song. "Song-based leitmotif, "song intonations" and "song-like quality" are discovered not only where these are legitimate by virtue of the character of the material, but also where song-like quality is totally absent as, for instance, in violin and piano concertos, the *Third Symphony*, etc. The critics who make these charges tend to juggle with terminology, to put it mildly. What they describe as "song-like quality" is very often Khrennikov's tuneful melodism, his cantilena-based musical thinking, the result of his free-flowing, generous melodic gift. On its own, this accusation would be a harmless enough terminological error but unfortunately such "interpretations" carry either a direct or, more often, implied (oblique) charge that the composer has allegedly

Khrennikov with one of his distinguished Soviet colleagues, Andrei Petrov.

borrowed a particular intonation or form from the realm of mass popular songs. In this way the critics seek to narrow down the intonational spectrum of Khrennikov's music, to attribute to it a kind of lowly, secondary quality. Who knows but that some of our music scholars have perhaps grown unused to the kind of generous melodic gift that Khrennikov so fully possesses!

If we were to discuss this aspect of Khrennikov's work at all, surely it would be more to the point to examine this song-like quality in the sense in which the composer himself has been using it. He writes: *Song-like quality, to my mind, should form the melodic basis of any composition by any composer, a basis which, depending on the musical genre, takes on specific, highly individual features. Far be it from me to seek to oversimplify things here. It is a fact that without a figurative melodic basis as transformed by the specificity of the particular genre the resulting composition, regardless of the expressive means used by its composer, would not be fully understandable, as it would lack that central element that finds a response in the hearts of music lovers. Not surprisingly, Mozart proclaimed: 'melody is the soul of music'. . . Prokofiev's work is based on melody throughout. What is really amazing in Prokofiev is that this melodic base so beautiful, so subtle and sincere is colored by an unmistakable national character regardless of form or genre. This is a classical example. Anyone who wants to understand the nature of the song-like quality of twentieth century music should start with Prokofiev's sonatas, symphonies, instrumental concertos, cantatas, operas and ballets.*

Similarly, Khrennikov's musical world rests on a melodic postulate—a vivid, graphic, and unhackneyed melodic image classical in its purity and always moving and memorable. Khrennikov has always been a gallant knight of melody and in this respect hardly any other twentieth century composer can match him. A. Kholminov was right when he wrote: *"It is precisely his melodies that determine the vitality of Khrennikov's compositions. The inexhaustible melodic richness is one of the more attractive aspects of his music and it seems to be rooted in some very fundamental intonational stratum . . . His melodies are always highly individual. Always pleasant, unaffected, and free of any pseudo-newness, they flow in a broad, full emotion-colored stream . . . It is this naturalness without oversimplification and primitivism, a naturalness with an inherent complexity, enhanced by talent and skill, that accounts for the depth of Khrennikov's compositions. From this springs the inalienable quality of his works, viz. their democratic thrust and message.* In this sense Khrennikov has never done anything that will cramp his style or stifle his own song, he never raped his talent, even in those days when melody was generally regarded (briefly, fortunately for us) as a hold-over from the past. His music is enjoying increasing popularity now that Soviet music, having overcome not a few obstacles and temptations in its evolution, is exploring new avenues for reaching out to the listener more effectively and is again turning its attention to eternal values and standards of beauty.

Khrennikov's emphasis on melodic expressiveness, the clarity of musical statement and lofty simplicity does not imply that he has stood aloof from the current trends in modern music or that he does not absorb, to refract through the prism of his original talent, new elements which enrich the compositional palette of the twentieth century. What is more, Khrennikov himself has made a significant contribution to this process of renewal and renovation, being aware that this is the only way to put his message across to his contemporaries. He has defined his fundamental position as follows: *Naturally a composer wishing to express his attitude to the problems of today's world cannot confine himself to the means discovered by his predecessors. But it is also true that only the content of his statement indicates the sort of means he should use. For a true artist, no means and methods are taboo. The important thing is to ensure that they have a definite and relevant direction. To express his idea embodied in a composition, the composer is free to draw on the entire cultural heritage of mankind both of the past and of the present. Undue emphasis on means of expression predictably produces a vapid and sterile result devoid of all living content and vibrant loftiness of art. All major composers in the history of music were innovators. For a truly forward-looking artist, content and form are always in organic unity and so he looks for his theme in art simultaneously with his search for expressive means by which to convey it.*

Throughout Khrennikov's career in music this quest has been very much in evidence. We may point to the highly original form and constructive treatment of his instrumental concertos, of the *First* and *Third Symphonies* (the Finale of the *Second Symphony* is anything but traditional); we may also recall his constant attention to renewal of his arsenal of technical devices, his orchestrations, notably his most recent scores. All this is perfectly natural for an artist who moves with the times and does not grow old in spirit.

Speaking of Khrennikov's innovative handling of musical form, we would like to stress one quality that has characterized his work over the past few decades—his laconic, aphoristic style of narration. This feature has been noted by critics in the past in the context of individual compositions. Some critics judged it positive, others negative. We believe this feature is of fundamental importance for the composer's dramatic thinking. Khrennikov addresses his audience directly, avoiding any devious ways, circumlocution or verbosity. This feature was apparent in his *First Violin Concerto* when it drew fire from some of the reviewers. This quality was very much in evidence in the *Cello Concerto*, which was immediately noticed by Rodion Shchedrin who wrote: *Once I was told by a fellow musician that the Khrennikov* Cello Concerto *is too laconic to the detriment of its imagery and that the concerto form always demands a broader concept and a greater measure of monumentality. I do not agree. There are no hard and fast rules or sacrosanct canons in creativity. The composer is free to choose a form and structure that are closest to his individuality. And I believe that Tikhon Khrennikov has been consistent in implementing his plan.*

As the years went by it became clear that, far from being a chance occurrence, it was the composer's policy, his clear-cut position, one that was fully consonant with the spirit of the times. Significantly, I. Martinov, one of the critics who complained in 1959 that Khrennikov's *Violin Concerto* was too laconic eight years later wrote about a style of narration that was *very terse, avoiding all that was superfluous, and added up to a clear-cut form.* For the *Third Symphony,* Martinov gave a more precise formulation: *It contains a good deal of information in condensed form. The composer seeks a precise and brief artistic utterance and this becomes a key element of his style.* This quality also contributes to the "audience accessibility" (to use one of Glinka's terms) of Khrennikov's

A scene from Khrennikov's opera for children, *The Boy Giant*.

music, enabling him to establish mutual understanding with the listener whose tastes change with the times.

A good example of Khrennikov's original approach to contemporary musical form is the way he solves the problem of finale, a key and challenging problem for any modern composer. The impression produced by significant compositions is often marred by cliché-ridden, sterotyped finales which come as an anti-climax, leaving us disappointed and fretting that the composer, having stated an interesting idea, has drawn a conclusion full of commonplaces. In this respect the finales of Khrennikov's post-war instrumental compositions present a stark and welcome contrast by virtue of their convincing logic, originality and optimism even when they have none of the traditional concluding bravura as for instance, in the *Second Piano Concerto* or the *Third Symphony*. Clearly, this is a result of the composer's great skill and his carefully thought-out dramatic concept. But there is even more reason to look for an explanation of the remarkable nature of Khrennikov's finales on the ideological-esthetic plane, rather than on the technological. The very cast of Khrennikov's gift, his world outlook, his social optimism, dictate to him a resolution of symphonic conflicts that invariably carries a message of a positive ideal. However, we should qualify this statement by saying that the essentially optimistic cast of Khrennikov's gift has tended, in the opinion of many critics and biographers, to overshadow all other features of his rich, emotional nature. Many critics, either forgetting or simply ignoring the high drama of some pages of the operas *In Storm* and *Mother*, and the *First* and *Second Symphonies* and of more recent works, began to portray Khrennikov as an one-dimensional, simple-hearted, naive poet of "simple and everyday human feelings and emotions", to portray him as an optimistic live-wire who looks at the world through rose-colored glasses. The bias of these critical simplifications and cliches is apparent to anyone with the slightest objective acquaintance with Khrennikov's scores. It is true that he is an optimist, full of joie de vivre and that a tragic view of reality is alien to him. In this respect he has been himself throughout his career in music. What is more, even in the late fifties and early sixties, when Shostakovich's tragedy-colored lead attracted a host of imitators, Khrennikov remained himself, true to his character and his world outlook. But this does not mean, repeat not, that Khrennikov turns his back on life's conflicts and disregards the burning problems of human existence, the human predicament. And the radiance of Khrennikov's finales is by no means an unclouded radiance, but the result of the composer's reflections on human existence which is also full of joy and not just drama, a life he believes in and in the name of which he creates his music.

This definite sense of purpose, wholeness and loyalty to himself, this blend of an innovative approach to composition and instant intonational recognition, coupled with the use of favorite devices drawn from his rich technological arsenal, all this enables us to speak of Tikhon Khrennikov's idiosyncratic style. This style is a component of the musical panorama of the twentieth century at what is perhaps the most productive and fruitful phase of its development. In the context of the motive factors and catalysts of the musical movement of our century, we often hear references to the important discoveries of the neo-Viennese school and of the technical innovations of the post-war years. But as we approach the end of the century the fundamental contributions of those who played "first fiddle" in the orchestra of world music become increasingly obvious. We are referring to those musicians who, while not eschewing new ideas and inventions, have drawn their chief inspiration from their observations of the passing scene, from life itself, who treasured eternal humanistic and esthetic values and ideals and who addressed their art to their fellow men. Prokofiev and Shostakovich, Myaskovsky and Bartók, Khachaturyan and Vladigerov, Britten and Orff, Honegger and Martinu, Barber and Villa-Lobos, Copland and Auric . . . We have every reason to add to this galaxy of classics of the twentieth century, with many of whom Tikhon Khrennikov has shared common creative principles and been linked by bonds of friendship, his name as well. All of them, each in his own way but always with the utmost sincerity and faithfulness, reflected their day in their music, and the life of their own people. It is this that brought them not only recognition but the grateful affection of millions of music lovers. . .

Bela Bartok (top) and Zoltan Kodaly (bottom), two of the galaxy of twentieth-century classical composers which also includes the name of Tikhon Khrennikov.

A GENEROUS TALENT

Tikhon Khrennikov is a worthy heir to the great Russian classical tradition. His music is always an expression of his inner world, his innermost feelings and emotions. We value highly his inspiration and professional skill. The audiences are invariably captivated by the natural sound and beauty of his music, a happy combination of talent and erudition.

Franco Mannino

Tikhon Khrennikov with two of his great contemporaries: Andre Jolivet and Dmitri Shostakovich.

For half a century now, Tikhon Khrennikov's music has been affording pleasure and enjoyment to millions of music lovers at home and abroad. The tremendous human appeal of his music derives from its expressive melodies and a refreshing novelty of treatment, the fruits of his ceaseless creative searchings. His symphonies, concertos, operas, ballets, instrumental pieces, incidental music and songs cast a spell over the audience.

For all its extroversion and accessibility, Khrennikov's music, like any other significant artistic phenomenon, is by no means simple to explain. If we were to list the qualities that have characterized his music down through the years and constitute the sum total of his unique style, we should mention first of all his wonderful gift for melody.

From the outset of his career, Khrennikov has been asserting the primacy and permanent value of melody as the foundation of good music. He has adhered to this principle in everything he wrote, producing works always brimful of fresh, vigorous and beautiful melodies.

Tikhon Khrennikov is one of the composers who have renovated the expressive means of twentieth century music. The melodic style and rhythm of his music are remarkably natural, unaffected and yet rich in discoveries and fresh approaches. His music is noted for that consummate simplicity which is the trademark of great art. His *Second Piano Concerto* with its essentially contemporary harmonies, vivid and plastic themes, overwhelming freshness and rich imagination is a shining example of this.

The melodic gift, daring, originality and keen sense of the present, inherent in Khrennikov's art, do not wholly explain the enchanting effect produced by his music. In addition, it contains qualities which defy description or precise musicological definition but which combine to make his music spontaneous and full of outgoing emotionality, so that even his most serious works find their way to the listener's heart.

Tikhon Khrennikov's contribution to Soviet and world music is great indeed. His opera *In Storm* is generally acknowledged as one of the works

in this form that constitute the foundation of the Soviet school of opera. His comic opera *The Low-Born Son-in-Law* is a masterpiece of the twentieth-century output in this genre. His recent ballets *Love for Love* and *A Hussar Ballad* have found a permanent place in the repertoire of European ballet troupes. His three symphonies and five instrumental concertos are performed by some of the world's best soloists and conductors while his incidental music is lending charm and a lavish touch to dozens of plays, films and TV productions.

Khrennikov's music was well represented at the Moscow Autumn-'81 festival by his *Three Pieces for Violin and Symphony Orchestra* dedicated to Igor Oistrakh, models of melodic ingenuity and classical harmony.

Every concert season brings fresh proof of the enduring popularity of Khrennikov's music.

The ovations aroused by the performance in countries around the world of his major works , some of them acknowledged twentieth century classics, attest to the composer's world renown.

We can hardly do better than conclude our story about Tikhon Khrennikov, composer and man, by quoting what Yuri Shaporin, one of the founding fathers of the Soviet school of music, once wrote about the composer: *In speaking of Tikhon Khrennikov, who is dearly loved by our people, the first word that suggests itself is Generosity. His is a generous talent, a generous heart, and a generous artistic personality.* Today, after a lapse of many years since this was written, we have pleasure in adding: his is an inexhaustible generosity.

Tikhon Khrennikov: a generous man dearly loved by his people.

The Principal Works of Tikhon Khrennikov

OPERAS

In Storm, libretto by A. Faiko and N. Virta based on N. Virta's novel
Loneliness   — 1939
2nd version   — 1952
Frol Skobeyev, libretto by S. Tsenin   — 1950
2nd version (entitled *The Low-Born Son-in-Law*)   — 1967
Mother, on a libretto by A. Faiko based on Maxim Gorky's novel of the
same name   — 1957
The Boy Giant, a children's opera on a libretto by N. Shestakov and N.
Satz   — 1969
Much Ado about Hearts (libretto by B. Pokrovsky after Shakespeare's
Much Ado about Nothing)   — 1972

OPERETTA

A Hundred Devils and a Girl, on a libretto by Y. Shatunovsky — 1963
Musical Chronicle
A White Night, libretto by Y. Shatunovsky   — 1966

BALLETS

Our Courtyard (Happy Childhood), libretto by N. Kasatkina and V.
Vasilyev   — 1970
Love for Love, libretto by V. Boccadoro and B. Pokrovsky after Shake-
speare's *Much Ado about Nothing*   — 1975
A Hussar Ballad, on a libretto by O. Vinogradov   — 1978

SYMPHONIES

First Symphony   — 1935
Second Symphony   — 1943
Third Symphony   — 1973

INSTRUMENTAL CONCERTOS

First Piano Concerto   — 1933
Second Piano Concerto   — 1972
First Violin Concerto   — 1959
Second Violin Concerto   — 1975
Cello Concerto   — 1964

CHAMBER MUSIC
Songs to words by Alexander Pushkin, Sergei Yesenin and Robert Burns;
Unaccompanied choruses to lyrics by Nikolai Nekrasov;
Pieces for piano and for violin;
Songs to words by Soviet poets

INCIDENTAL MUSIC TO PLAYS
Much Ado about Nothing by W. Shakespeare;
Don Quixote after Miguel de Cervantes;
Long Ago by A. Gladkov, and others

FILM MUSIC
At Six P.M. after the War; The Train Goes East; A Hussar Ballad; the Miners of Donetsk; True Friends; Ruslan and Lyudmila; Duenna; The Captain's Daughter and others.

Index

Page numbers set in *italics* refer to illustrations.